How To Choose Your Bible Wisely

Preface

During 1982–83 the *Harvester* magazine carried a series of fourteen articles entitled 'Translating the Bible into English'. These were revised for publication in 1985 as *Bible Translations and How to Choose Between Them*. Reviews of this book were received from many journals (see list at the beginning of the Bibliography), as well as a few letters sent to the publisher; all such views and suggestions have been taken into account for this revised edition.

The remaining stocks of the book were destroyed by fire in 1990; but, more importantly, several more revisions and new English translations of the Bible and of the New Testament have been appearing since 1985; some attitudes to versions have also been changing or hardening, some towards, and some away from, the views expressed in the earlier edition. Having further thought over various issues during the period, my views have also undergone development. So the present book, founded on the previous one, has not only a different title, but substantially improved content.

Acknowledgements

Since the previous book, I have received encouragement for the new edition from Tim Carr and Jeremy Mudditt, as well as from Paul Ellingworth who offered many detailed suggestions.

My wife, Matilda, has carefully read through the whole draft and made many useful suggestions. I am indebted to her for her invaluable support.

The work has been carried out during part of the sabbatical leave granted by the University of Ghana.

Contents

1

Opening up the question

1.1 THERE IS ONLY ONE VERSION, IS THERE?

Moslems have always had a fundamental reluctance to translate their scriptures and prayers out of the Arabic language (Sanneh); for them, there is only one scripture —in the original Arabic.

The Christian Old and New Testaments were respectively written in the Hebrew and Greek languages, while Jesus himself probably spoke Aramaic in a Roman colonial environment. Nevertheless, for many centuries, the Catholic Church in Europe also had a fundamental reluctance to translate the Bible and their liturgy out of the Latin language; for them, there was only one scripture —the Latin Vulgate (Sannch). So, right up till the fourteenth century, there was no whole-Bible translation into English at all!

Nowadays, those who have little contact with the Christian faith may be aware of only one version of the Bible: the one that is always bound in black, carried by church-goers. This is the version with the distinctive 'Bible English', which sounds impressive as a literary monument of the past.

Some churches use a written liturgical form of service, with the result that their readings from the Bible have to harmonize with these liturgies; so the Anglicans use the King James Version and the Catholics now use the New Jerusalem or the New American Bible. So again, for many

11

Anglicans and for Catholics, there seems to be only one version in regular use. Those who think that every nation should have its own national church also require that there should be one national version of the Bible [van Bruggen, p.145–7].

Those churches which came into existence as a result of the Protestant Reformation at first strongly preferred the Geneva Bible. But nowadays such wholehearted allegiance has been transferred to the King James Version, which is said to be the product of 'an age of faith'. Indeed, some less-informed church members imagine that the 'St James Version', as they call it, is the original Bible! Contrary to the wish of its translators, it

> 'has become crystallized and frozen in the minds of so many as to be God's last word, if not God's only word, to his people.' [Jones, p.14–15]

With an attitude like that, every other Bible version over the centuries becomes automatically a 'corruption', if not 'perversion', of that 'original'!

Some leaders of churches, fellowships, ministries and Christian organizations, especially newly-founded ones which seem vibrant and growing, tend to make constant use of that Bible version, thereby giving such a strong impression to all members that those who wish to be recognized as fully-approved in that social group must use that same version, at least during meeting or service times.

So, for a number of different groups of people, whether by lack of information leading to ignorance of the issues involved, or by formal or informal pressure to conform to the norms of a social group, some minds have already been closed on the question of 'which Bible to choose?'.

1.2 THE ANSWER IS EDUCATION, IS IT?

Since hardly anybody can read the Bible in the Hebrew, Aramaic, and Greek originals of the Bible, a programme of education in these languages could be instituted for all Christians to enable them to do so! But that would be beyond the reach of most Christians of any educational level and would make intellectual achievement into a prerequisite for spiritual growth. A teaching programme like this is what Moslems regularly mount for their members all over the world who are not Arabic speakers. It may also have happened in some places where Christian missionaries from Europe taught their converts English or French so that they could read the Bible in these languages. But your ability to learn languages should have no bearing at all on your ability to grow as a Christian.

It has, however, seriously been proposed that Christians, especially new believers, should be educated into the archaisms and intricacies of a Bible version like KJV so that they can understand the full traditional terminology of the Christian faith. Again, this puts an intellectual brake on spiritual progress which is entirely unnecessary in view of the wide variety of English versions of the Bible currently available to suit every educational level.

1.3   TOO MANY VERSIONS, ARE THERE?

Those who had little interest in the Christian faith precisely because of that forbidding black book with its archaic English may find that the same Book can actually be both attractive in cover and appealing in language, as soon as some other version is brought to their attention.

Serious Christians, however, are very well aware that there is more than one version of the Bible and especially of the New Testament. Even in the seventeenth century, at least ten versions existed in addition to KJV.

But how many are aware that today there are nearly sixty more or less different English versions of the whole Bible (see Table 1 below); plus another seventy-five or so of the New Testament (see Table 3)? Many of these are still available at least in second-hand bookshops; a dozen or two are currently available in Christian bookshops and a few also in some secular bookshops.

Some might say that the multiplicity of new versions

is due to the fact that too many publishers are jumping on the bandwagon merely for commercial profits. Therefore, some may turn away from contributing to these profits and stick to the version they have been used to. It is no doubt true that publishers find it profitable to bring out many attractive editions even of the same version for slightly different markets. But there must be very few versions, if any, which were created solely for the profit motive.

Likewise, hardly any of the versions were created solely to bolster or justify a particular theological or denominational point of view, although evangelicals, modernists, Catholics, liberals, and Jehovah's Witnesses, have all been accused of doing so.

1.4   TO IMPRESS US, OR TO EXPRESS HIMSELF TO US?

In the Bible, is God seeking to impress us with the majestic Hebrew, Greek, or archaic English languages and with the great literature to be found in the Bible, as in Old Testament times when he appeared in the earthquake, the storm, and the fire, in order to make his people tremble in adoration? [Kraft, p.21]

Or is God expressing himself to us in his word, the Bible? If you believe that the Bible is indeed God's word to humanity, then that must mean that God is communicating with us.

In Old Testament times, 'they read from the book of the law of God clearly, made its sense plain, and gave instruction in what was read.' (Neh. 8:8 REB) The Bible can be known from childhood onwards, and is expected not merely to be understood, but also to be obeyed (Jos. 1:8; Matt. 28:20). 'Everything in the Scriptures is God's Word. All of it is useful for teaching and helping people and for correcting them and showing them how to live.' (2 Tim. 3:16 CEV) 'See, the Word of God is alive! It is at work and is sharper than any double-edged sword . . . it is quick to judge the inner reflections and attitudes of the heart.' (Heb. 4:12 Stern) The Christian message is no longer a mystery concealed as in the pre-Christian era, but rather a mystery revealed (Eph. 3) both in the living and in the written Word of God.

'The KJV translators said: 'Without translation into the [popular] tongue, the unlearned are but children at Jacob's well (which was deep) without a bucket or something to draw with.' [Kubo & Specht, p.21] It was to enable ordinary English-speaking people to respond to God's deep message that Wyclif and, later, Tyndale risked their lives to claim the Bible out of Latin into the English language.

1.5 CHOOSING IGNORANTLY OR WISELY?

If you do not know the original languages of the Bible, how can you judge which version is good or bad, or merely better or worse than another? How can you choose a Bible for yourself or your family wisely, rather than in comparative ignorance of the issues involved? If all versions are equally good, or all equally bad, it would hardly matter; but all versions are not equal!

You can look at the cover and the size of the Bible; and you can look at the layout of the pages. You can read the claims made for the version by the publisher on the book jacket, in the introduction, or in an advertisement. You can read what various respected Christian leaders have said in favour of, or against, that version. But how do you really make up your mind and 'choose wisely'?

Are older translations better, or newer ones?

Who were the translators—how many and from what denominations? Are they true believers? Are they academics or amateurs?

What Greek manuscripts of the New Testament do they use?

Do they translate word for word, or meaning for meaning?

Is the English idiomatic or strange, archaic or modern?

For what educational level is the version intended?

Does it matter if you 'like the way this particular verse is rendered' in some version?

Many different criteria, mostly linguistic ones, must be taken into account in any proper evaluation of Bible translations. And these criteria vary greatly in importance, as we shall see.

Table 1: *Whole Bible translations*
(in chronological sequence)
All (2/3-letter) labels to be used later for reference, whether derived from *Author* or from *Title*, are in **bold** type. (For convenience, all such labels can also be found in the Index.)

Author, Editor, (Publisher), ...	Date(s) of Publication [main year(s) in **bold**]	Title [+ comments]
J **WYC**lif 1, Nicholas	1380 /**82**	(from Latin, extremely literal)
J **WYC**lif 2, J Purvey	1384 /**88** /90	(from Latin, quite free)
W **TYN**dale	**1525** /34 /51	—
M **CO**verdale	**1535** /37	(from Tyndale)
J Rogers	**1537** /51	**MAT**thew Bible (from Coverdale)
R **TA**verner	**1539** /52	(from Matthew)
M Coverdale, T Cranmer	**1539** /40 /69	**GRea**T Bible (from Matthew)
Whittingham	1557 /**60** /76 /1602	**GEN**eva Bible (from Tyn, Mat & Grt)
M Parker	**1568** /72 /1606	**BI**shops' Bible (from Grt)
Allen, Martin, Bristow, Reynolds	1582/1**609–10**	**DOU**ay-Rheims (from Latin)
—	1**611**/27/38/1762/69	**K**ing James Version = **A**uthorised version
A **PUR**ver	**1764**	A New and Literal Translation
R **CHA**lloner	1738 /50 /63 /**72**	(revisions of Douay)
B Mac**MAH**on	**1783**	(revision of Challoner)

C THOmson	1808	(from Greek OT and NT)
J MacRAE	1799/1815	. . . an interpretation after the Eastern manner
B BOOthroyd	1817/24/36/**53**	—
S SHArpe	1840/**65**	—
Julia SMIth	18**76**	—
(Cambridge)	1881/**85**	Revised Version
J N Darby	1871/**90**	A New Translation
R YOUng	1862/**98**	A Literal Translation
—	19**01**	American Standard Version (from RV)
J B ROTherham	1872/19**01–3**/13	The Emphasized Bible
F FENton	1890/19**03**/10	Holy Bible in Modern English
(American Bible Union)	1864/19**13**	—
J MOFfatt	1913/28/**35**	A New Translation
E J GOodspeed, J M P smith	1923/27/31/**35**	An American Translation
S H Hooke	1941/**49**	The Bible in Basic English
(Nelson)	1946/**52**/66/**71**(89)	Revised Standard Version
R KNOx	1945/**49**/55	(from Latin)
G M LAMsa	1940/57	. . . from ancient eastern manuscripts
(Watchtower)	1950/**61**/71	New World Translation
A B Traina	1950/**63**	The Holy Name Bible
F E Siewert (Zondervan)	1958/**65**	The AMPlified Bible
A Jones (Darton LongmanTodd)	19**66** (85)	Jerusalem Bible
G Verkuyl (Zondervan)	1945/59/**69**	New Berkeley Version = Modern Language Bible
Confraternity of Christian Doctrine	1941/**70** (86)	New American Bible
(Oxford, Cambridge)	1961/**70** (89)	New English Bible
(Lockman)	1963/**71**/77	New American Standard Bible (from ASV)
K N Taylor (Tyndale)	1967/**71**	The Living Bible Paraphrased
S T Byington (Watchtower)	(1943) **72**	The Bible in Living English

Author, Editor, (Publisher), ...	Date(s) of Publication [main year(s) in **bold**]	Title [+ comments]
A EDIngton	**1975**	The Word Made Fresh
W F BECk	1963/75/**76**	The Holy Bible in the Language of Today
(Bible Societies)	1966/**76**/92	Good News Bible = Today's English Version
(N Y International Bible Society)	1973/**78**	New International version
J P Green Sr	1971/**82** (87)	King James 2 Version
(Nelson, Nashville)	1979/**82**	New King James Version (=RAV)
(Bagster)	**1982**	Revised Authorised Version (=NKJ)
H Wansbrough (Darton L. T.)	19(66) **85**	New Jerusalem Bible (from JB)
Confraternity of Christian Doctrine	19(70) **86**	New American Bible: revised NT (from NAB)
J P Green Sr	19(82) 84/**87**	Literal Translation of the Bible (from KJ2)
World Bible Translation Center	1978/80/**87**	Easy-To-Read Version = English V for the Deaf
(Worthy/Word)	1983/86/**88**	The Everyday Bible = New CentV. = Int Child B
(Oxford)	19(52) **89**	New Revised Standard Version (from RSV)
(Oxford, Cambridge)	19(70) **89**	Revised English Bible (from NEB)
B Hurault (Philippines)	**1990**	Christian Community Bible
J P Green Sr	1962/**91**	Children's/Teenage/Modern King James V.
(Bible Societies)	1991/**95**	Contemporary English V./ B. for Today's Family

Table 2: *Old Testament translations*
(in chronological sequence)
All labels to be used later for reference, whether derived from *Author* or from *Title*, are in **bold** type.

Author/Editor/ Publisher	Date(s) of Publication [main year(s) in **bold**]	Title [+ comments]
Benisch	**1856**	–
Friedlander	**1884**	–
Spurrell, H	**1885**	–
Margolis (Jewish Publication Society of America)	**1917**/55/ (85)	The Holy Scriptures
(Jewish Publication Society of America)	1962/73/82/**85**	Tanakh: New Jewish Version

Table 3:
New Testament translations
(in chronological sequence)
All (4-letter) labels to be used later for reference, whether derived from *Author* or from *Title*, are in **bold** type.

Author, Editor, (Publisher), ...	Date(s) of Publication [main year(s) in **bold**]	Title [+ comments]
D **Mace**	**1729**	(revision of Douay)
R **With**am	**1730**	–
W **Whis**ton	**1745**	Primitive New Test.
R **Wynne**	**1764**	... carefully collated with the Greek ...
E **Harw**ood	**1768**	A Liberal Translation
J **Wors**ley	**1770**	–

Author, Editor, (Publisher), . . .	Date(s) of Publication [main year(s) in **bold**]	Title [+ comments]
J **Wesl**ey	1745/68/**90**	revision of KJV
G **Wake**field	1791/**95**	–
T **Hawe**is	1**795**	. . . with a view to assist the unlearned . . .
W **Newc**ome	1**796**	An attempt towards revising our English trans.
N **Scar**lett	1**798**	–
W **Willi**ams	1**812**	A modern, correct, and close translation
W **Thom**son	1**816**	–
Doddridge, Campbell, McKnight	1760/**1818**	–
Belsham?	1**819**	NT in an improved version (from Newcome)
R **Dick**inson	1**833**	Corrected version of the Christian scriptures
G **Penn**	1**836**	The New Covenant
(E **Tayl**or)	18**40**	Revision of the AV with aid of other translations
A **Camp**bell	1826/**48**	(from Doddridge)
J **Tayl**or	1852–4	The Emphatic NT according to the AV
H **Hein**fetter	1854–7	A literal translation . . . and an English version
L **Saw**yer	1**858**	. . . with chronological arrangement . . .
H **High**ton	1**862**	–
H **Alf**ord	1**869**	(from KJV)
R **Ains**lie	1**869**	–
G R **Noy**es	1**869**	–
J **Bow**es	1**870**	. . . translated from the purest Greek . . .

S **Davidson**	/18**76**	
W B **Crick**mer	18**81**	The Greek Testament Englished
J W **Hans**on	18**84–6**	The New Covenant
J **Joyn**son	18**92**	–
J **Murdo**ck	1850/**93**	(from Syriac)
R D **Week**es	18**97**	The New Dispensation

J **Moff**att	19**01**	The Historical NT
—	1898/1901/**04**/09	The **Twen**tieth Century New Testament
A S **Worr**ell	19**04**	–
S **Lloy**d, G W Moon	1904/**05**	The AV of the NT in 'revised English'
W B **Godb**ey	1902/06/**23**	(from Sinaiticus)
f s **Ball**entine	1901/**09**	Modern American Bible
R F **Weym**outh	1902/03/**09**	NT in Modern Speech
E **Clar**ke	19**13**	The Authorised Version Corrected
H T **Ande**rson	19**18**	. . . from the Sinaitic manuscript . . .

H B **Mont**gomery	19**24**/54	Centenary Translation of the NT/in Modern Eng
A E **Over**bury	19**25**/32	The People's New Covenant Scriptural Writings
G N **Lefe**vre	19**28**	The Christian's Bible NT
J A **Robe**rtson & al.	1924/**29**	(from Weymouth)
E E **Cunn**ington	1914/19/**30**	(from KJV and RV)
w g **Ball**antine	1923/**34**	Riverside NT
G W **Wade**	19**34**	The Documents of the NT . . .
I **Pan**in	1914/**35**	. . . as established by Bible numerics . . .
C **Latt**ey & al.	19**35**	**West**minster Version
J **Greb**er	19**37**	A New Translation and Explanation . . .
W W **Mart**in	19**37**	. . . critically reconstructed and retranslated
F A **Spenc**er	19**37**	(from Greek by a Catholic)

Author, Editor, (Publisher), . . .	Date(s) of Publication [main year(s) in **bold**]	Title [+ comments]
c b Williams	1937/50	The NT in the Language of the People
R M **Wils**on	1938	The Book of Books . . .
E L **Clem**entson	1938	—
Confraternity of Christian Doctrine	1941	(from Challoner, replaced by NAB 70)
(J **Smith**)	1867/1**944**	an Inspired Revision of the Authorized Version
G **Swan**n	1**947**	—
T R & R E **Ford**	1**948**	Letchworth Version in Modern English
C B **Pers**hall	1**951**	. . . The Authentic Version
c k Williams	1**952**	A New Translation in Plain English
J A **Kl**eist & J L **Lilly**	1**956**	(from Greek by Catholics)
H J **Sch**onfield **1**	1**956**(85)	The Authentic New Testament (by a Jew)
J L **Toma**nek	1**958**	NT of Our Lord and Savior Jesus Anointed
j b Phillips **1**	1**958**/60(72)	The NT in Modern English
O M **Norl**ie	1951/**61**	Simplified NT in plain English for today's reader
Th S **Noli**	1**961**	(Albanian Orthodox NT)
K S **Wues**t	1956/59/**61**	An Expanded Translation to clarify text of AV . . .
A E Knoch	1919/26/44/**66**	**Conc**ordant Literal NT
W **Barc**lay	1**968**	A New Translation

G H **Ledy**ard	**1969**	Children's NT = New Life NT
A **Cress**man	**1969/71**	The NT in Worldwide English
j b Phillips **2**	**1960/72**	The NT in Modern English
British & Foreign Bible Society	**1966/73/77**	The **Trans**lator's NT
J E **Adams**	**1977**	Christian Counsellor's NT: in Everyday English
S L Morris (Internat. Bible Pub)	**1978/80/81**	The **Simple** English Bible: New Testament
R **Latt**imore	**1982**	Four Gospels, Revelation, Acts & Letters of Apostles
H J **Sch**onfield **2**	**19(56)85**	The Original NT
H W **Cass**irer	**1989**	God's New Covenant.
D H **Stern**	**1989**	Jewish New Testament
McCord	**1989**	NT Translation of the Everlasting Gospel
Andy **Gaus** (Phanes)	**1991**	The Unvarnished NT
R W Funk ed. (Polebridge)	**1990–**	**Scholars** Version **Trans**lation of the NT
E H **Peter**son	**1993**	The **Message:** NT in Contemporary English

Who Translates What?

2

Who are the translators?

2.1 WHAT SKILLS DOES A TRANSLATOR NEED?

If you think carefully about the process of translating, you will realize that quite a few different skills seem to be needed [cf. Foster, ch. 1].

He (or she) needs to have competence in expressing meaning in the destination language, commonly called Target, or Receptor, language (TL). As far as we are concerned, this requires mother-tongue competence in English, a skill that has been recognized for Bible translators only in the last few decades.

He needs to be competent also in the Source Language(s) (SL) and cultures. In the case of the Bible, this requires competence in Hebrew, Aramaic, and Greek.

He should have specialist knowledge of the content of the documents being translated. These latter two scholarly skills have usually been the only pre-requisites for appointment as a Bible translator.

He should also understand the linguistic theory of translation and have had practical experience in translating. This is a skill that some translators seem to have possessed intuitively, but has only rarely and recently been recognized as a pre-requisite.

2.2   HOW MANY INDIVIDUALS?

From the above it should be immediately obvious that no single individual is likely to possess all the required skills.

So, if one individual undertakes to translate the Bible, he or she cannot help manifesting all his or her strengths and weaknesses, including pet theories, uncompensated by interaction with any fellow-translators (as in YOU, FEN, Schonfield, Gaus, Green, Taylor).

Of course, a single translator might possess several of the skills (eg. JND, MOF, jbP, Cass, Stern); while a whole group of translators may still lack the full complement of skills and proceed rather like the blind leading the blind! But both these latter possibilities are in principle unlikely. So we generally expect that one-person translations will be inferior to those produced by organized groups of translators.

As the first draft translation of each book of the Bible is likely to be made by a single translator, a translation panel for each of the two Testaments is likely to consist of only between ten and thirty individuals, who meet periodically to review and comment on each other's drafts.

Outside this panel which is directly involved in translating, several experts may be consulted for guidance in specialist areas, like Near-Eastern languages and cultures, archaeology and geography, botany and zoology, etc.

At a later stage, experts in English style may be invited to review and improve the draft translations.

Then, beyond these inner and outer circles of actual contributors, an indefinitely large number of church representatives and others (like 'all English-speaking Bible Societies' for GNB and CEV) may receive copies of the draft translations, partly for reasons of public relations, and partly to solicit comments especially on sensitive church-related issues, perhaps for experimental usage in Bible study groups. But contributions from this last group are likely to be minimal as the officials contacted are usually preoccupied with quite different issues.

In all cases, the final decision as to what goes into the final version normally rests with the inner core group of actual translators, even though a Bible society or a Christian or secular publisher ultimately sponsors its publication and distribution. [Wonderly, ch. 9; Nida, Towards, pp.245–51; Good News, ch. 4; Nida & Taber, pp.99–104]

So, whether the number of translators claimed for a Bible version is between 10 and 30, like RSV, GNB, TEB, NRS; or between 50 and 60, like KJV, NAS, NAB; or more than 100, like NIV, NKJ, [Foster, p.18] it may actually not make too much difference, bearing in mind what has just been said, so long as the number is more than one.

2.3   FROM WHAT COUNTRY?

Though some translations explicitly claim to be 'American' (ASV, GOS, NAS, NAB), none of these seems to be so American as to be strange to me as a non-American.

But some translations do occasionally reveal their specific country of origin more or less clearly: whether Scotland, eg. 'factor' (Lk. 16:1 MOF); or England, eg. 'Whitsuntide' (1 Cor. 16:8 NEB, but not REB with 'Pentecost') [Kubo & Specht, p.34, 158–9]; or USA, eg. 'twenty dollar bills' (Lk. 10:35 LBP) 'stinger, stomped' (Rev. 9:10; 14:19 CEV). Translations whose country of origin is clear to all presumably suit those who live there, but equally tend to put off those who do not; and the latter always form a majority of the world's English-speaking population.

So the most desirable translation is surely one which is suitable for mother-tongue speakers of English in Britain, North America, Australia, etc, as well as for second-language speakers in Africa, India, etc; perhaps with both British and US editions, differing only in the matter of spelling. Those versions which seem to have

the most 'international' English would seem to be GNB
and NIV.

2.4 OF WHAT DENOMINATIONAL AFFILIATION?

All one-person translation teams automatically belong to
only one denomination:

> Messianic Jewish: Stern (which includes hebraized proper
> names and many Hebrew technical terms); Orthodox: Noli;
> Mormon: Smith; Christian Science: Overbury.

But some larger teams also belong to only one denomination:

> Jehovah's Witnesses: NWT, which is certainly not 'filled
> with the heretical doctrines of this cult' [Fee & Stuart, p.41],
> even though a few aberrations can be found;
> Calvinist: GEN with its copious and extreme anti-catholic
> notes; Lutheran: TYN;
> Roman Catholic: all versions include the deuterocanonical
> books (as KJV also did) and sometimes have different verse
> and psalm numberings from protestant versions; DOU had
> very Catholic notes; DOU, CHA, KNO used spellings of
> names like 'Sophonias' (= 'Zephaniah'); NAB and NJB's
> Catholic affiliation can occasionally be detected in footnotes.
> An Episcopalian bias can also be found in the KJV with
> 'bishop' and 'church', compared with Tyndale's 'overseer'
> and 'congregation'.

In the same way as more than one translator is better
than just a single one, the translators should have more
than one denominational affiliation among them—indeed,
as many as possible; so that a single denomination's
views, especially on sensitive issues, should not prevail
over other possibilities, or even be written into the
translation itself.

Larger teams of translators will invariably have members
from more denominations (eg. KJV, NAS, NIV, NKJ, NRS,
REB), whether or not the members are actual representatives of these denominations. If there is denominational
balance among translators, the Bible will not be translated
in such a way as to favour any one denomination as
opposed to another; and so their translation of the Bible

can be used as a real touchstone by which to continually test any denomination or church's beliefs and practices which are supposed to be subject to biblical authority.

2.5 HOW SERIOUSLY DO THEY BELIEVE THE BIBLE MESSAGE?

Barclay said: 'Ideally, the translator's mind should be in perfect unison with the mind of the author whom he seeks to translate, even to the extent of sharing, or at least entering into, the experience of the author.'

No one can translate the Bible well unless he believes that it has to do with real relationships between God and mankind; and that its message is to be taken seriously, indeed as a matter of life and death.

Those with what has been called a 'liberal' view of the Bible and the Christian religion are likely not to regard the Bible text as quite as sacrosanct as others of a more 'conservative' leaning. The result may be that emendations of the manuscripts may be more readily accepted, as well as rearrangements of the text, editorial additions or interpolations (as in Ps. 72:18–9 MOF), even to the extent of printing in a different typeface the supposed different documents composing the Pentateuch (MOF; CCB); and footnotes may also tend in the same direction. One also wonders about the NT translations of Schonfield, a Jew, and that of Gaus ('Unvarnished'). Where such translations are relatively word-for-word, there is little scope for 'liberal' ideas to get in to the wording; but where the translations are relatively free or meaningful, the risk of such ideas getting in is much increased [Foster, p.78–9]. Nevertheless, contrary to what one reads in certain pamphlets and booklets, it is very rare indeed that a somewhat ambiguous original meaning is deliberately translated in such a way as to deny a miracle or the deity of Christ, or to break the NT fulfilment of an OT scripture; whenever that seems to be the case, there is almost always a manuscript or other linguistic reason to be found.

On the other hand, I would expect that 'conservatives',

or 'evangelicals', are more likely to contain within their ranks translators with the fullest empathy with the biblical message, regarding it as sacrosanct, and believing and practising it in their own daily lives.

Not that such empathy guarantees a perfect Bible translation, because it is quite possible to write in to the Bible translation some doctrines, including correct doctrines, which are not original at that point in the Bible. AMP constantly overloads the text in this way, while NBV shows a similar perspective in its footnotes.

The following illegitimate equivalences are made [Epp]:

	in LBP:	for the common:
in Rom. 2:21–2	get to heaven	eternal life
	way to heaven	righteousness
	if we trust Jesus Christ to take away our sins	faith
	by coming to Christ	believing
and in Titus 1:5:	pastor	elder

NIV has also been accused of harmonizing OT passages (eg. Ps. 2, especially v.12; Isa. 7:14 'virgin') to suit the NT fulfilment. Evangelicals may like such Bible versions, just because they happen to share the same theological bias as the translators; but all such biases are to be deplored as changes to the original meaning of the Bible.

SUMMARY

In this chapter, we have looked at the the four broad skills that translators need and have concluded that such skills are much more likely to be found in an organized group of translators, rather than in a single individual, who are members of several denominations, rather than just one. Although those of 'evangelical' convictions generally take the Bible message most seriously, such convictions should never be written into the translation itself.

3

How well do they know the original languages?

Most readers of the Bible in English know nothing of the original Hebrew, Aramaic, and Greek languages, and very little of these cultures except what they can gather from the Bible itself.

Indeed, a few translators of the Bible have also not used the original languages, but have either translated from the Latin Vulgate (all Catholic versions till this century) or have paraphrased an earlier English version (LBP, Cres) (see ch. 4).

Some Bible translators may have had little formal instruction in the biblical languages (FEN, Byington in BLE, Twen); yet BLE is the only one to correctly transliterate 'Sheth' and 'Jepheth' (Gen. 5–6)! But, in general, there is no doubt that we expect translators of the Bible to be up-to-date in their knowledge of the original languages and cultures and related issues, so that they can appreciate the full original meaning of the biblical texts before venturing to translate them.

3.1 OLD TESTAMENT

A certain amount of Judeo-Christian cultural background has been absorbed over the centuries into general European civilization. However, increasingly during the twentieth century, archaeologists and other investigators have continued to uncover all sorts of information about the Near-Eastern way of life in past centuries: of nomads and townspeople, of patriarchs and aliens, about the flora and fauna, on agriculture and trade, on the geography and history of the various peoples, and about cultural and religious practices.

Some geographical names can now be translated more accurately, for example (Thompson):

Deut. 11:24
RSV: the western sea;
GNB: **the Mediterranean Sea in the west**

Ezek. 47:18
RSV: the eastern sea;
GNB: **the Dead Sea.**

Gen. 31:21
GOS: the River;
GNB: **the River Euphrates.**

Isa. 11:11
KJV: Cush; RSV: Ethiopia;
GNB: **Sudan;** NRS: **Nubia**.

Some obscure Hebrew words have had their meanings clarified:

Lev. 3:1ff
RSV: peace-offerings;
NIV: **fellowship offerings;** NRS: **offerings of well-being;**
REB: **shared-offerings.**

2 Sam. 1:21
RV: fields of offerings;
REB: **showers on the uplands.**

Lev. 26:3
KJV: images; RV: sun-images;
GOS: **incense altars.**

Prov. 26:23
RV: silver dross;
GOS: **glaze.**

Whole passages full of obscure technical terms, eg. from mining (Job 28) or from astronomy (Job 38), have become clearer and clearer from RV to RSV and from NEB to REB.

Sometimes the newer knowledge has enabled a choice to be made between variations in the original manuscripts.

Sometimes, however, no evidently correct solution has been provided, but the number of plausible possibilities has merely been increased:

1 Sam. 1:24
RV: three bullocks;
RSV: a bullock, three years old.

Deut. 15:18
REB, NIV, NJB: twice; GOS, GNB, RSV: half.

Eccl. 3:11
KJV: world; NAS: eternity; REB: past and future; NJB: passage of time; NAB: the timeless; MOF: mystery; GOS: ignorance.

From investigations into other ancient Near-Eastern languages, Semitic poetry, including Hebrew poetry, has come to be better and better understood. So has the grammatical usage of prepositions, and even the pronunciation of the divine name YHWH as 'Yahweh' though only ROT, CCB and NJB have had the courage to use it.

A few translators, working on their own, have made mistakes. Young consistently mistranslated the perfect and imperfect aspects of the Hebrew verb throughout the Old Testament; similarly, Knoch, with his consistent mistranslation of the Greek tenses (Conc). And Fenton mistranslated the very first word of the Bible as 'by periods' (plural) and even defended it in a footnote! [Bruce]

Occasionally we find two variants side by side in a version, but this is not recommended, because the original writer did not intend both variants:

Isa. 52:15, 'startle *and* sprinkle', Isa. 19:18, 'city of the Sun *or* Destruction', both AMP. [Gordon]

Although there is no question that the increasing knowledge of Near-Eastern languages and cultures has helped Bible translators, from KJV to RV to RSV to REB, to make better sense of several obscure Old Testament words and passages, there are still many places, especially in books like Job, where uncertainties as to meaning make all translators resort to conjecture. One can see this in some of the footnotes in some versions. And the study of the structure of Hebrew discourse may be expected to offer further improvements in future OT translations.

3.2   NEW TESTAMENT

Let me start with a suggestion that the GEN New Testament (1602 edition) is the only correct version of Matthew 11:29 that I have found (now also CCB):

> 'Take my yoke on you, and learne of me *that* I am meeke and lowly in heart: and yee shall find rest vnto your soules.'—the aorist imperative verb 'learn' seems to me to require an object clause introduced by 'that' for the Greek *hoti*.

However, it is only in this verse that this very old version seems to me correct.

It was at the end of the last century that the rubbish dumps of Egypt and elsewhere yielded up to investigators large quantities of 1st-century AD papyri, written in a Greek not unlike that of the New Testament, about all kinds of everyday matters. That was when it became clear that NT Greek was not some special kind of 'divine' Greek, even though it was clearly not the classical literary Greek of the 5th–4th centuries BC either. In fact, the NT was written in *koine* (common) Greek. This incidentally gives us a clue as to what kind of English might be appropriate for its translation (ch 12.3).

In Matthew 6:2, most versions have something like: 'they have (got) their reward (already)'; but now we understand that the Greek verb involved was used in commerce for 'having an invoice paid in full' (Jones, p. 35). As it happens, the translation does not actually need to change.

But, in other cases, there should indeed be a change:

Acts 16:12
KJV: part;
RV: district.

Acts 6:2,5; 15:12,30
KJV, RV: the (whole) multitude (of the disciples);

GNB: **the whole group (of believers);** REB: **the whole company (of disciples);** NRS: **the whole community (of disciples).**

Acts 10:30
Gk: 'from fourth day';
GNB, NJB, REB: **three days ago.**

[Báez-Camargo, p. 439–40]

Once it is understood that the Greek language has two aspects, one for an action viewed as *progressive* or as habitual (Lk. 11:9 'ask . . . seek . . . knock'; Gal. 6:1 'restore'), the other for a *single* action, however complex, viewed as a whole [Gross], then we can expect much more sensitive translations of tenses as we already have in some of the more recent versions:

progressive
Jn. 20:17
KJV: touch me not;
NAS: **stop clinging to me;** GNB, NIV: **do not hold on to me.**

Matt. 3:14
KJV: forbade;
NIV: **tried to deter.**

Acts 4:34
RSV: sold;
GNB: **would sell.**

Lk. 5:6
KJV: brake;
RV, NKJ, RSV: **were breaking;**
NIV (NRS): **began to break.**

single action
Matt. 14:30
GNB NIV: was afraid;
NAS: **became afraid.**

Throughout this century, further investigations have been going on into the multilingual background of the New Testament, with Hebrew and Aramaic, as well as Greek and Latin, all playing a role. Scholars have also investigated possible poetic structures in Matthew, John, some Letters, and Revelation (see especially NAB, NJB).

SUMMARY

No Bible translators before the end of the nineteenth century had access to as much knowledge of the original languages and cultures as we have today. Therefore, the most recent translators are the most likely to be rightly informed as to the true meaning of the original, provided that they include experts in these matters (CEV, REB, NRS, NAB, NJB, NIV, GNB, NAS; JPSA, SCVT).

But some obscurities still remain. Preachers should never base a whole sermon on one verse (eg. Eccl. 3:11!) as it is found in one translation.

However, the above examples of improved translations of words show that they are usually of relatively little spiritual importance. And only a few verses here and there, out of thousands, are affected at all. So the overall effect of the new knowledge of languages and cultures is remarkably slight.

4

What originals do they translate?

4.1   NOT THE ORIGINAL LANGUAGES

Those who think that the original Bible is the King James/
Authorised Version (in English) assume that all later
versions must be corruptions of that 'original Bible', and
so would reject them on principle!

Some recent versions (NKJ=RAV, KJ2=LTB, MKJ) are
more or less modern-dress paraphrases of KJV. So is LBP
paraphrased from ASV, and Cres from RSV.

From the sixteenth century till about 1960, the Roman
Catholic Church officially recognized only the Latin
Vulgate, translated in the fourth century AD by Jerome,
as authoritative, so that all English translations had to be
based on this Latin original (DOU, CHA, KNO; Conf). The
very first English Bible translations, made by Wyclif and
his associates, were also made from the Latin since they
did not know any Greek or Hebrew. Lamsa translated his
version from the Syriac.

In all these cases, we have English translations of
English or Latin or Syriac translations of the original
Hebrew and Greek manuscripts; and this inevitably involves additional risks of failing to transfer adequately
the full meaning of the originals.

4.2   'HOLY SCRIPTURE AS ORIGINALLY GIVEN'

If circumstances were ideal, you might imagine that the
Bible translator takes up the original Hebrew and Greek

paper hand-written by Isaiah or by Paul, and translates it! But actual circumstances are very far from ideal.

No such 'autographed' written material now exists. All that we now have are hand-written copies of copies of copies of copies . . . . . . of the original 'autographs'; and sometimes the copies are only fragmentary. Naturally, the shorter the time between the original writing and the now-existing copy (because fewer other copies will have intervened), the better that copy is likely to be. That is why older copies are normally to be preferred to later copies. [Edwards]

Down the centuries, manuscripts, once recognized as authoritative, were meticulously copied by real professionals. But we should remember that all these manuscripts were without punctuation, and even without spaces between words; and the commonest words were regularly abbreviated to speed up the work.

Sometimes a single copyist made one copy of a manuscript lying open in front of him, so that accidental, unintentional errors in copying might be due to his eye missing out some word or line, or falling on the same word or line twice. Comments left in the margin by a previous copyist might have got incorporated into the copy (eg. in Lk. 9:54, 'as Elijah did' is added in some manuscripts).

Sometimes, however, one person would read aloud from a manuscript for several copyists to copy simultaneously, so that copying errors might also be due either to misreading or to mishearing. (In 2 Cor. 8:7, the variants 'your love for us' and 'our love for you' probably came about because the Greek words for 'you, your' then sounded like those for 'us, our'.)

Copyists were so familiar with the Bible, that unintentionally, or even intentionally, they tended to 'harmonize' one Bible passage with another similar one. (In Mark 1:14, the unusual original 'the gospel . . . of God' has had 'of the kingdom' inserted, probably from Matthew.)

They also tended to correct, clarify, or 'improve' any awkward or unusual words or passages in the interests of completeness and readability. (In Mk. 1:2, the original 'in Isaiah the prophet' came to be 'in the prophets' because more than Isaiah is actually quoted.)

Any such intentional changes in copying could be made either by orthodox believers trying to strengthen some doctrine, or by heretics trying to weaken some doctrine with which they disagreed. On either side, of course, they were guilty of changing the original meaning.

Therefore, it should be clear that the older copies, with the fewest opportunities for either kind of change, should generally be preferred.

Some people assume that the oldest English version of which they are aware, the KJV of 1611, being nearer to the time of the original writing of the Scriptures, must therefore be based on Hebrew and Greek manuscripts which are older than those on which more modern English versions are based. But is that true?

The oldest Hebrew manuscripts of parts of the Old Testament date from the third to the first centuries BC; and when did these come to light for biblical scholars and translators? In the 1940s and 1950s.

The oldest Greek manuscripts of parts of the New Testament date from the first to the third centuries AD; and when did they come to light for the use of Bible translators? In the 1890s.

Therefore, through no fault of the KJV translators, they simply had no access to these two sets of very old manuscripts, but had to translate from the later manuscripts which were then available to them.

Several evangelical doctrinal bases include, as part of the article on the inspiration and infallibility of the scriptures, some phrase like 'as originally given', which means 'as written by the original authors under the inspiration of the Holy Spirit before any copying of these manuscripts or any translating into other languages'. But how can we now have access to the scriptures 'as originally given'? Since the existing copies of Bible manuscripts differ from each other in innumerable smaller, and several larger, details, how can we ever get back to the texts 'originally given' for translators to translate?

If a translator were to look at just one single copy, he would inevitably find a few errors peculiar to that copy— which he would then have to translate! But nowadays translators always compare different copies of the original to see where there may be variations which would affect their translating.

Of course, they do not have all the thousands of manuscripts lying there in front of them! Rather, they rely on editions of the Hebrew Old Testament and of the Greek New Testament, in which manuscript experts have compared the existing copies and have judged which variants are most likely to have been those originally written, by printing the Hebrew or Greek texts including these variants, together with footnotes laying out the evidence for all the variants.

These are known as 'critical editions' which embody the scientific results of 'textual criticism'. Here, 'criticism' means 'judgment' in a legal or scientific sense, and not 'attack' (on the Bible) as some writers erroneously think.

Where there is some genuine doubt for manuscript reasons as to whether a particular word or passage was 'originally given' or not, the doubt could be indicated by [[. . .]] as used by NRS; NAB uses [. . .].

Some scholars and translators go beyond what has just been described, and venture to rearrange sentences and paragraphs and even chapters to conform to what they consider to have been the original arrangement. Eg. MOF in various groups of verses in Jn. 3, 7, 10, 11, 12,15;16, 18; NAB; NEB Isa. 5:24–5 › 10:4+; JB, REB Job 41:1–6 › 39:30+. But there is rarely any evidence from the manuscripts for this and it is best avoided.

4.3 OLD TESTAMENT

The various books of the Old Testament were composed at different times and were written down over several centuries. By the beginning of the Christian era, the Old Testament was written with only the consonants (as is still the case in modern Hebrew newspapers). It had been copied and re-copied with infinite care down to about the ninth century AD, when Jewish scholars, known as the Masoretes, fixed the written text, introducing spaces between words and vowel signs (to facilitate pronunciation now that the language was no longer spoken everyday). This is the standard Hebrew Masoretic Text (MT), on which all translations mainly depend. [Bascom, Review of Tov, ch. 2]

However, wherever that text is unclear, translators may think of an alternative division of words. Eg. in Hos. 6:5, 'my judgment goes forth as the light' (NRS, GOS), instead of 'thy judgments are as the light that goeth forth' (KJV).

Translators may also think of alternative vowels to go with the originally-given consonants. Eg. in Jer. 49:1, 'Molech' (GNB) or 'Milcom' (NRS, NJB), an Ammonite God, instead of 'their king' (KJV) (*Hebrew *malkam*).

Beyond these possibilities within the Hebrew tradition, translators who found difficulty with the Masoretic Text could also consult very ancient versions made from the Hebrew text long before it was standardized: especially the Greek Septuagint (2nd century BC), the Syriac (2nd/3rd century AD), and the Old Latin (2nd/4th century AD). For example, in Gen. 4:8, 'Let us go out to the field' is added to the Hebrew on the strength of several ancient versions; in 1 Sam. 8:16, because of the Greek version, we have 'cattle' in NIV, GNB, NRS, GOS, rather than 'young men' KJV (the Hebrew words being similar); where the Greek version has more material than the Hebrew, as in Jer. 25, NJB puts it in brackets, while REB has it in footnotes.

From the middle of this century, however, fragments

of Hebrew manuscripts about one thousand years older
than the standard MT were discovered at Qumran; these
are known as the Dead Sea Scrolls, and shed some new
light on Isaiah, Habakkuk, and parts of most other OT
books.

In Hab. 1:17, thanks to a Scroll, we may have 'Are they
going to use their swords for ever . . .' GNB (REB), instead
of 'Shall they therefore empty their net . . .' KJV (NRS).

In Isa. 33:8, 'its witnesses/oaths' NIV/NRS; instead of
'the cities' KJV.

NRS ends 1 Sam. 10 with four extra sentences from a
Scroll. [Omanson, NRS]

In most cases, however, the Dead Sea Scrolls have
tended to confirm the Masoretic Text in places where
some scholars had tried to emend it.

In addition to adjusting the Hebrew MT vowels and
word-divisions, referring to the Dead Sea Scrolls, and
consulting the ancient versions, translators are still sometimes forced to make some conjectures as to the possible
meaning of some obscure words or phrases. Conjecture
is avoided as much as possible in NIV, GNB, jpsa, while
NEB, NAB, MOF tend to indulge in it too much.

MOF and CCB also indulge, without any manuscript
justification, in printing with different type-faces the
'source documents' of the Pentateuch according to one
scholarly theory of its origin; such a theory also turns up
in the notes of NJB and NAB.

4.4   NEW TESTAMENT

With the New Testament, the situation is rather different
because, from the first three centuries of the Christian era,
almost a hundred papyrus fragments of the NT survive;
nearly all of these have come to light during the twentieth
century.

Two fourth-century manuscripts (*codices*), called
Sinaiticus and Vaticanus, came to light in the nineteenth
century, in time for RV=ASV. The fifth-century Alexan-

drinus manuscript came to light only in the sixteenth century, but was neglected by scholars till the following century. These three all represent an *Alexandrian* type of text, and turn out to have thousands of, mostly minor, differences from the Byzantine type (mentioned below).

A *Western* type of text is represented by the fifth-century Greek 'Codex Bezae' and by ancient versions in Latin and Syriac.

After the Roman emperor Constantine proclaimed Christianity as the official religion of the Roman Empire in the fourth century, an Eastern or Byzantine type of text arose at Constantinople (or Byzantium), eventually comprising a family of over 5000 manuscripts and continuing till the fifteenth century. This large family of manuscripts is also termed the 'majority' text.

One twelfth-century manuscript from this family, along with a few others, was used by Erasmus, the scholar who produced a new edition of the Greek New Testament in 1516, which was to form the basis of KJV in 1611. The 1633 printing of this edition by Elzevir was advertised as the 'received text', that is, 'the text which is now received by all' scholars of the mid-seventeenth century. [Macleod]

There is much less evidence that the first- to third-century papyri or the fourth-century manuscripts, which tend to have shorter readings, were 'corrupted by heretics', as some have alleged, than that the many later Byzantine manuscripts, which tend to have longer 'harmonized' readings, were 'improved by the orthodox'.

All Bible versions till the nineteenth century, including KJV, CHA, YOU, inevitably had to make do with the only Greek manuscripts and ancient versions known by that time; but more recently KJ2=LTB, NKJ=RAV, MKJ have gone back to the same basis. Towards the end of the nineteenth century, RV, ASV, JND tended to make the maximum use of the newly-discovered manuscripts.

In the present century, 'critical editions' of the Greek New Testament, weighing the evidence of the papyri and of the manuscripts of all text-types, have been prepared by experts, with the result that most recent versions are based on such a Greek text, though some versions may make their own 'eclectic' decisions on manuscript variants as they arise.

Those who do not understand such 'critical editions' of the Greek text mock it by calling it something 'pieced-together' which never really existed (CLW 4:2, p.2). They think they are doing better by following the 'majority text', which of course equally does not exist in one document!

Many verses of KJV result from copyists' harmonizing one passage with another similar passage. For example, the 'Lord's Prayer' in Lk. 11:2 KJV has been filled out with material from Matt 6:10 where it properly belongs according to the older manuscripts (see NIV); in Col. 1:14, 'through his blood' KJV is added from Eph. 1:7 where it belongs; in 1 Cor. 11:29 'unworthily' KJV has been imported from 11:27 where it belongs; Acts 9:5–6 KJV has been harmonized to 26:14; Matt. 27:35 KJV has a long addition taken from Jn. 19:24; in Matt. 5:44 KJV has two phrases added from Lk. 6:27.

The word or phrase mentioned is not found *at these points* in the older manuscripts (and therefore not in most modern English versions); but it is in fact found in all manuscripts somewhere.

More seriously, however, some phrases or short passages do not appear at all in some of the older manuscripts and so not in most versions, except those that follow the later manuscripts on which KJV was based.

For example, Matt. 6:13 KJV, NKJ included the doxology to the Lord's Prayer, originally added from 1 Chr. 29 for liturgical convenience, but not in the older manuscripts; similarly, Acts 8:37, found in KJV, YOU, NKJ, LBP, NBV; in Rom. 1:16 'of Christ' KJV has been added from sixth, eighth, and ninth-century manuscripts; 1 Jn. 5:7, according to NKJ, can be found only in fifteenth-century Greek manuscripts and the Latin Bible! Interestingly, AMP prints these additions to the original in italics.

At the end of all the Pauline letters, only GEN and KJV add notes about the writer and/or the place from which it was sent, which information is to be found only in the very late Greek manuscripts underlying these versions.

Other variations between the KJV type of text and most modern versions include: Jn. 10:16a: 'fold' KJV (and Latin) is replaced by 'flock' TYN, NKJ; in 1 Tim. 3:16: 'God' KJV, YOU, NKJ occurs, it is claimed, in hundreds more Greek manuscripts than the alternative 'who' (the Greek originals are almost the same in form), but these hundreds all date from the eighth century onwards and come from the same area, while all the ancient versions from different areas as well as the two oldest manuscripts had the other alternative, as do most modern versions; some insert 'Christ' though the strict antecedent of 'who' is 'God', so that in any case the theological difference between the two manuscript alternatives is minimal!

Most of the arguments about the Greek manuscripts (on which an English version is based) boil down to a preference either for the *older manuscripts* followed by most modern versions, or for the *later manuscripts* followed by KJV and others (which seem to have been padded with pious 'improvements' of the originals). It is grossly dishonest to pretend, as some have, that such modern versions have been 'shorn of essential Christian doctrines' [CLW 1.1 p.32]: all essential doctrines can be found in all versions.

SUMMARY

In much of the Old and New Testaments, the origin-ally-given readings can be found by normal 'textual criticism' of the existing manuscripts with varying degrees of probability. Most of the recent English versions take the best account of such findings; those which do so, and yet do not also indulge in unnecessary conjectural emendations, are NIV, GNB, NAS, NRS, REB.

Wherever there are problems with translating the original manuscripts, there should be 'textual' notes in the margin (or at the foot) of the page. [Osborn] The absence of textual notes from versions like GOS, LTB, TEB gives a misleading impression of unanimity.

However, having just devoted several pages to this issue regarding the manuscript originals, we have now to say that the overall effect on a whole Bible version is rather limited. This is especially so in the Old Testament, but even in the New Testament only an estimated 3% is affected at all, while as little as 0.001% have substantial variants. [Sheehan; Foster p.16] It is therefore a gross distortion of the whole truth to pretend to judge a Bible version as either 'genuine' or 'counterfeit' merely because it is, or is not, based on a particular type of Greek NT manuscript!

Preachers and teachers should learn the same lesson as in ch.3: not to base a whole sermon, and certainly not a whole doctrine, on any one verse of Scripture, least of all one that is not supported by the weight of manuscript evidence.

Is It Translated Accurately?

5

Crossing over from one language to another

5.1 THE LANGUAGE SPECTRUM

You may view language as consisting of nothing but writing, ignoring speech. Or you may view it as consisting of nothing but words, ignoring sentences.

But a more realistic view of language is diagrammed in Figure 1, as a sort of iceberg. Only the tip of the iceberg is visible above the surface of the water, and with icebergs and with languages alike there is much more below the surface.

On the surface of language, we either hear speech or see writing.

When you turn the dial of your radio, you will hear different stations speaking many different languages. If they are speaking Chinese or Swahili, then you can hear their sounds, but can understand nothing; for you, it is just sounds, the tip of the iceberg, with nothing underneath. However, if French, German, or Spanish is the language spoken, you can still hear the sounds, and you may even catch a few words here and there, depending on where you may have been for your holidays! But, if the language being spoken is English, you still hear the sounds of course, but you also catch every word and sentence, and understand the whole meaning being expressed—without even thinking about it! In other

51

Figure 1.

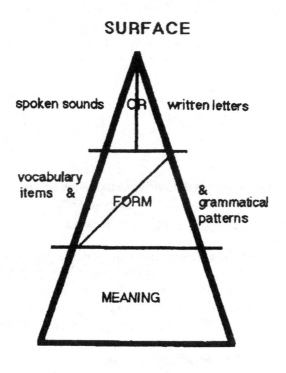

words, when your own language is being spoken, there is far more to that language than mere sounds.

If you get a postcard from friends on holiday abroad, you will see some words printed on the card and on the stamp. If the writing is in Greek, Hebrew, Arabic, or Russian, you can see it, but understand nothing. If the writing is in French or Spanish, you can still see it, and can also read the words with some kind of pronunciation, and even understand some of them. But if the printing is in English, then you see, you read, you understand everything, without even thinking about it.

So, in the case of a language we do not know, we hear only sounds or see only marks written on paper, but nothing more. If you have ever studied any foreign language, you may recall how you gradually came to recognize more and more words and grammatical patterns as you progressed. However, even quite advanced students, having puzzled out the meanings of individual words with the help of a dictionary, may still feel they do not understand what the whole passage actually means. In the case of our own language, however, whether spoken or written, we hardly even notice the sounds or the spelling, nor do we pay much attention to the individual words and grammatical patterns, unless there is some kind of mistake; rather, we go straight for the meaning, the bottom section of the 'iceberg'—after all, that is what really matters.

A meaning is expressed with an appropriate wording which in turn is expressed with an appropriate spelling or 'sounding' (Halliday, p.21; cf. Nida, Towards, ch. 3). The spelling and the sounds are accessible to anyone with normal eyes and ears; but the full meaning is accessible only to those who know the particular language all the way down through its layers.

We could compare meaning to the goods displayed for sale in a shop, what the shop is there for; while the spellings, sounds, words, and grammatical patterns are like the shop's windows, shelves, stands, and counters, which are all needed for the shop to operate, but are not what it is there for.

What has just been outlined is the inherent three-layer nature of every human language, past or present, for whatever purpose it may be used.

5.2 UNITS OF LANGUAGE

If you know only how to write English, then you may think that all languages are and were written with the same units: letters of the alphabet; words with spaces between; clauses with commas; sentences with capital letters and full stops; indented paragraphs; chapters; books.

Figure 2

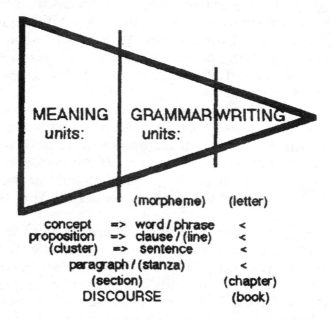

		(morpheme)	(letter)
concept	=>	word / phrase	<
proposition	=>	clause / (line)	<
(cluster)	=>	sentence	<
		paragraph / (stanza)	<
		(section)	(chapter)
		DISCOURSE	(book)

But the original Hebrew and Greek manuscripts (and most of their copies) were written with only the letters of the alphabet written continuously from the beginning to the end of the particular book of the Bible. In other words, there were no spaces between words, no capital letters, no punctuation marks. It was only the physical edges of the writing surface which made the copyist stop one line and start a new one!

Because of our familiarity with dictionaries which tell us about words, many of us think that the word is the principal, if not the only, unit of grammar as well. But a little recollection of your study of grammar at school, helped by a glance at the centre bottom of Figure 2, may remind you that there are grammatical units larger than the word: words may combine into phrases and into clauses (simple sentences); and clauses may combine into compound or complex sentences.

Each of these grammatical units expresses meaning

only indirectly. The mental concept (or idea) of a thing or an event may be referred to by a word in some language or by a larger phrase in another language. But people do not communicate with each other one word at a time. The 'thought' or 'information' or proposition about some state of affairs may be communicated by means of a clause (or a line of poetry). A cluster of propositions may be combined in a sentence or in a paragraph (or a stanza of poetry). Paragraphs can be combined to form sections of the whole discourse (like one book of the Bible).

When 2 Tim. 3:16 says 'Every Scripture is God-breathed . . .' (KJ2) or 'All Scripture is given by inspiration of God, . . .' (RAV), it must be understood to apply originally only to the Old Testament, but now primarily to the Scripture as a whole, and so to each Testament and to each book, with each book's sections and paragraphs, expressing clusters of propositions, in turn expressing groups of concepts. Inspiration guarantees the veracity of revelation whose content (meaning) is communicated in writing. [Beekman, Idiomatic]

5.3   CROSSING OVER NEARER THE SURFACE

Figure 3 below suggests that one could cross over from Language A (in the case of the Bible, that is Hebrew, Aramaic, and Greek) to Language B (in our case, that is English) at any of the layers of the languages.

So, across the upper layers, we would expect to replace all the letters of the Hebrew and Greek alphabets with English letters, slightly modified. Mark 1:4, for example, would then look like the following:

Egeneto Iōannēs baptizōn en tēi erēmōi kai kērussōn baptisma metanoias eis aphesin hamartiōn.

Although the English speaker can now at least read the Greek aloud, this is still a Greek sentence filled with Greek words and hardly any meaning gets across at all. So this is not translation, but transliteration.

Figure 3

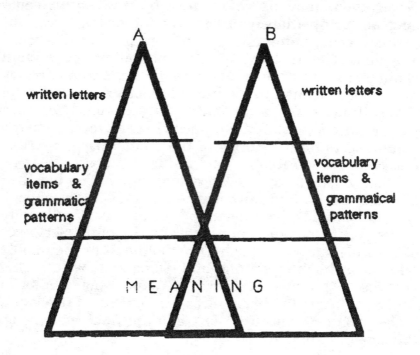

Moving down to the middle layer of the languages, that of vocabulary items and grammatical patterns, is it possible to cross over from one language to another here?

Let us try it for Mark 1:14–5 (Kingdom, with hyphens added):

> And after the to-be-given-over the John came the Jesus into the Galilee and preaching the good-news of-the God and saying that Has-been-fulfilled the appointed-time and has-drawn-near the kingdom of-the God; be-you-repenting and be-you-believing in the good-news.

This is obviously much better than the previous attempt, because now every Greek word, however complex it may be, has been represented in the same order by an English word or hyphenated phrase; but is it actually an English sentence? How much meaning can you get from it? This type of crossing-over from language to language is known as interlinear 'gloss', or colloquially as 'crib' or 'pony'. These are ideal for students learning foreign languages, including Greek or Hebrew.

Continuing with the middle layer of language, is it still possible to cross over, matching Greek words with English words, but now adjusting the word order?

And after *the the* John *to-be-given-over* the Jesus came into *the* Galilee and preaching the good-news of-*the* God and saying *that* The appointed-time has-been-fulfilled and *the* kingdom of-the God has-drawn-near ; *be-you-repenting* and *be-you-believing* in the good-news.

Apart from the ten italicized items, the resulting English of this fairly easy piece of Greek can nearly be understood with a certain amount of good will. But could this method of crossing-over be applied equally to a difficult piece of Greek, of which there are many examples, especially in Paul's letters?

The above are fairly extreme examples of crossing-over between languages towards the surface of language, especially between the smallest units of the middle layer, namely, words: giving us a word-for-word or literal translation which closely follows the linguistic forms of the other language in what is called formal correspondence. Confusingly, van Bruggen calls this type both idiomatic (p.153–4) and idiolect (p.67), indicating that he does not really understand the issues involved.

To further illustrate how much of an obsession word-for-word correspondence has become for some 'translators', I quote from CLW 4.2 of 1992, largely written by J P Green. In Mark 6:21, his Literal Translation of the Bible has:

'And a suitable day having come, when Herod on his birth-feast made a supper for his great ones, and the chiliarchs, and the first ones of Galilee.'

While NIV, according to him, has: '^ ^ ^ ^ [Finally the opportune time] came. ^ On his birthday Herod ^ ^ ^ [gave a banquet for] his ˆˆ [high officials] and ˆ [military commanders] and the leading [men] of Galilee.'

Green states that NIV has added 13 words (those in brackets) of their own; while 11 of the 22 Greek original words (those indicated with ˆ) are left untranslated. 'There is no correspondence with the Greek they are supposed to be translating. ... At every word, almost, God and the NIV translators disagree on this verse.' (p.9)

After quoting 2 Tim. 3:16, Green says: 'Scripture is made up of words, and all those words were individually God-breathed. ... Now men come along and replace those words that God breathed out with words that they have chosen, ... But God will not be mocked, and He will judge those who presumed to replace HIS God-breathed words with THEIR man-breathed words.' (p.6)

Green evidently thinks it was just words that God breathed, but not clauses, sentences, paragraphs, discourses, and indeed the whole of Scripture! He should be reminded 'not to dispute-about-words for nothing useful, to the casting down of those hearing.' (2 Tim. 2:14 KJ2 hyphens added).

The KJV translators had this to say: 'For is the kingdom of God become *words* or syllables? ... Add hereunto, that niceness in words was always counted the next step to trifling.' (my emphasis)

5.4   CROSSING OVER AT THE DEEP END

In terms of Figures 1 and 3, 'the deep end' refers to the bottom of the diagrams: where the meaning is located.

'As literal as possible, as free as is necessary' (RSV, NRS) is a good slogan for translators to follow, where it is understood that one translates as literally or word-for-word as possible (provided that the full original meaning is thereby preserved), and that one translates as freely as is necessary (to preserve the full original meaning, without adding any extra meaning). In other words, wherever there is any conflict of interest between the two, closeness of form is less important than faithfulness of meaning

[Wendland]. It would be irresponsible of any translator to translate word-for-word where readers of that translation would receive either a wrong meaning, or no meaning, or an obscure meaning (not in the original) [Fehderau, Quality].

'Almost any scholar can produce a literal rendering of the original languages. But this is only the *first* step in the translation process. Two important questions must still be asked: "*What do the words mean?*" and "What is the most accurate and natural way to express this meaning in contemporary English?" ' [CEV preface, my emphasis]

When the meaning of a word or sentence is not perfectly obvious, it may be understood in different ways by different people. To find out the meaning of Bible passages as intended by the original author, translators themselves or other scholars use exegesis to get the best principled interpretation of that meaning, compared with other alternatives.

This has nothing to do with any private interpretation which someone might wish to impose on a Bible passage, and is totally to be deplored in a translator. [Hess]

Incredibly, van Bruggen demands translation without exegesis! (p.106)

If a pupil is asked by the teacher to paraphrase a passage, he/she is expected to re-express the same meaning in his/her own words, both passage and paraphrase being in the same language. We find five Greek paraphrases of the same meaning in Matt. 3:11; Mk. 1:7; Lk. 3:16; Jn. 1:27; Acts 13:25. [Beekman, Idiomatic]

It is unfortunate that the word 'paraphrase' is popularly used for a meaningful translation which is so loose or free that it does not faithfully express the full original meaning!

Figure 4 is a diagram of the process of translating with the translator sitting in the middle.

He first faces to the left to confront a text in Language A—even though it seems upside-down and beyond com-

Figure 4

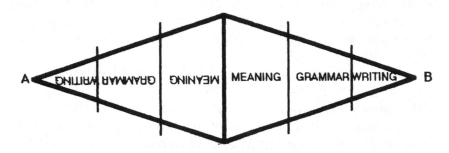

prehension to the lay person! The translator can read its written form; he can cope with all its grammatical patterns and knows its vocabulary; and ultimately comprehends its full meaning.

The translator then turns and faces to the right, which is Language B. In order to express that same meaning, he seeks equivalent grammatical patterns and vocabulary in Language B, and eventually writes it all out in the appropriate spelling.

He 'is stating the *meaning* of the text in such a way as to enable the readers of the translation to gain an understanding of the text similar to that of the original message.' [Arichea, Theology, my emphasis] He seeks 'to convey faithfully from one language to another the *meaning* intended by the original author' [Foster, p.11, my emphasis]

While the meaning expressed in the two Languages must be identical, the wording and the spelling of the two Languages are inevitably not identical. So it is only at these latter two layers of language that restructuring has to come in.

A travesty of this normal translation procedure is offered by J P Green in his numerous productions; eg. from SGT Perspective 1993, p.1: 'The concept that the Bible should be predigested by Scholars, and spit out in another form, is straight from Satan.' Every Christian translator knows that this description is itself a lie!

So what is being advocated here is basically a meaning-for-meaning translation, matching wherever possible with the vocabulary and grammatical patterns of the original languages, provided the full original meaning is preserved. This is accurate or faithful meaningful or communicative translation.

To call such a translation 'paraphrase' is very unhelpful because paraphrases also express the same meaning as each other, but in the same language.

Such translation has also been termed dynamically equivalent or functionally equivalent, but the former term especially can be construed so much in terms of equivalent response by the reader of the translation that the original meaning might even be adjusted a little to that end, which is of course totally unacceptable. [Andersons, p 3–4; Carson, Limits]

It is important to guard against the risk of over-adjusting towards the potential readers of the translation: For example, in 1 Ki. 20:11, 'Don't count your chickens before they hatch!' (LBP) [Foster, ch. 4] is over-adjusted, compared with 'The time for boasting is after the battle (REB, cf. GNB), and 'the man who puts on his armor should not boast as much as the man who ‹lives long enough to› take it off.' (ETR), and 'Do not let him that girds on boast himself like one who takes armor off.' (KJ2)

5.5   WHICH TYPE OF TRANSLATION?

If you are one of the very few who have in mind to learn the original languages of the Bible, then an interlinear translation is very desirable, at least to help that intention on.

If you are one of the few who have in mind to study the ancient biblical cultures and especially to do word studies of English biblical terms, then a close word-for-word translation is obviously desirable. But to know what it means, one is dependent on commentaries or college lecturers or learned preachers; and it is certainly possible for the less-educated to be misled by preachers who also may not actually know what it means, but have more imagination! Because such translations use the traditional theological terms, their use is sometimes taken as a badge of orthodoxy in certain theological circles.

The first Wyclif version was word-for-word as a 'transcription of God's law-code in the Vulgate', while the second Wyclif version was 'translated after the sentence (sense), not only after the words' [Bruce, review of Duthie].

But for almost all Christians, including those just mentioned, a faithful meaning-for-meaning translation, indeed probably more than one, would greatly facilitate their day-to-day reading of the Bible as God's word.

And for those who are not Christians at all, a meaning-for-meaning translation would seem to be indispensable as an evangelistic tool.

But how are we to know which translation is which? Does it help us to decide if it is called a 'Bible' or a 'Version' or a 'Translation'? Briefly, it does not help, though some say that 'versions' are produced by committees, while 'translations' are produced by one person.

Translation type	Called 'Bibles' 'Testaments'		Called 'Versions'	Called 'Translations'
Word-for-word	BLE BBE NAB	NASB= NKJB=	RV=ASV KJV=AV KJ2= MKJV NRSV NASV RSV RAV NBV	YOU LTB JND NWT
Meaning-for-meaning	NJB NEB JB LBP AMP	REB TEB=ICB GNB= BTF=	NIV =NCV ETRV TEV CEV	GOS MOF

'I have a picture in my mind of what translation is like which is very helpful to me. I imagine the events and truths of the Bible as a wonderful scene which is taking place in the middle of a great field. All around this field are the people of the world, watching this scene from their own homes. . . .

Now it is an ordinary thing in our experience that, without turning our head or looking in a different direction, we can focus our eyes on different things. If I am looking at something through a window, I can study it very carefully without ever thinking about the window at all. On the other hand, it is also possible to focus completely on the window, and to notice the little cracks and specks of dust, and not to pay any attention to what is going on outside. *A good translation is like a good window.* If we want to focus on how it is done, we can. We may see that there are very few flaws, that it is smooth and even. But most people do not want to think about the translation itself, any more that they want to study a window. They want it for what it shows them on the other side. They want to be able to read it and see the truth it talks about. If the translation they are reading is not done clearly and naturally, it is like a poor window, cracked or warped or uneven. When you look at something through a window like that, the thing looks so strange that you are forced to think about the window itself, whether you want to or not.' [Mundhenk, my emphasis]

'Translation it is
that opens the window, to let in the light;
    that breaks the shell, that we may eat the kernel;
that puts aside the curtain, that we may look into the
    most holy place;
    that removes the cover of the well, that we may come
        by the water.'
                    [KJV, quoted in CEV; my division into lines]

6

A hundred versions of Hebrews 1:1–3

EXPLANATION

To convince everyone that innumerable different translations of these few verses have been made, they are displayed below so that you can see for yourself exactly what they are like. Much the same meaning is conveyed by each of the versions, which means that they are paraphrases of each other. They vary considerably in how closely they stick to the original words, and how much they expand to convey shades of meaning.

First comes the transliterated Greek followed by an interlinear gloss. Then the versions are arranged more or less in chronological order (including the original KJV*); occasionally two editions of the same version appear in the same line, with the variants separated by /.

Each line is identified on the left with a two- or three-letter label for whole Bibles (see ch. 1, Table 1) and a four-letter label for New Testaments (see ch. 1, Table 3); a final 1 or 2 means 'first' or 'second' edition. (All these abbreviations can also be found in the Index.)

The symbol [ ] means a paragraph or line break. Underlining, bolding, italicizing, capitalization, all belong to the version quoted, along with ‖ . . . ‖, ‹ . . . ›, / . . . /, [. . .], (. . .), —, and other punctuation.

Extracts of these verses from various versions can also be found in Macgregor, appendix 1; and in Dennett, Problems, p.20–2.

Table 1   Hebrews 1:1

GRK	**polymerōs kai polytropōs palai ho theos lalēsas tois patrasin en tois prophētais**
k.i.t.	*in-many-parts and in-many-manners of-old the God having-spoken to-the fathers in the prophets*
WYC1	Manyfolde & many maners sumtyme god spekynge to fadris in prophetis
WYC2	God, that spak sum tyme bi prophetis in many maneres to oure fadris,
TYN	God in tyme past diuersly and many wayes, spake vnto the fathers by prophetes:
COV	God in tyme past dyuersly & many wayes, spake vnto the fathers by prophetes,
GRT	God in tyme past diuersly and many wayes, spake vnto the fathers by Prophetes:
GEN	At sundrie times and in divers maners God spake in the olde time to our fathers by the Prophets:
BIS	God which in tyme past, at sundry tymes & in divers manners spake unto the fathers in the prophetes, []
DOU	Diversely and many waies in times past God speaking to the fathers in the prophets:
KJV*	God who at sundry times, and in divers manners, spake in time past unto the Fathers by the Prophets.[]
Whis	God, who at sundry times, and in divers manners, spake in time past unto the fathers by the prophets,
PUR	God having spoken many times and many ways of old, to the Forefathers by the Prophets; []
Wynn	God, who at different times, and in various manners, spoke of old time to the fathers by the prophets,
Harw	God, who in antient time spoke to our ancestors by the prophets at various times, and in various manners,
Wors	God, who at sundry times, and various ways, spake of old unto the fathers by the prophets,
CHA	God, who at sundry times and in divers manners spoke in times past to the fathers by the prophets,
Wesl	God, who at sundry times and in divers manners spake of old to the fathers by the prophets,
Hawe	God, who spake to the fathers of old at various times, and in different manners by the prophets,
Newc	God who, in several parts, and in several manners, formerly spake to our fathers by the prophets,
Scar	God, having spoken at different times, and in various ways formerly to the fathers by the prophets,
THO	God, who in sundry parcels and in divers manners spake in time past to the fathers by the prophets,

Will	God having formerly addressed the Fathers, through the Prophets, in sundry Shapes and in various Modes,
RAE	God, who hath at many times, and in various manners of old, spoken to the fathers by the prophets,
Thom	In several portions, and in several ways, of old, God having spoken to the fathers by the prophets, []
Dodd	God, who in sundry parts and in divers manners, anciently spake to the fathers by the prophets,—
Bels	God, who in several parts and in several manners formerly spake to our fathers by the prophets,
Dick	God, who, in various divisions, and in different modes, anciently communicated to the fathers by the prophets,
Penn	God, who at various times, and in various manners, spake to the fathers formerly by *his* prophets, []
Camp	God, who in ancient times spoke often and in various ways to the fathers by the prophets,
Tayl	God, who in sundry parts, and in divers manners, spake in time past unto the fathers by the prophets,
Hein	God, who at sundry times and in divers manners, spake in time past unto the fathers by the prophets, []
BOO	In various parts and in various manners God spoke formerly to the fathers by the prophets;
SHA	God, who at many times and in many manners spake in time past to the fathers by the prophets,
Sawy	God, who at many times and in many ways spoke anciently to the fathers by the prophets,
High	God, who at sundry times and in divers manners spake in time past unto the fathers by the prophets, []
Ains	God having spoken in times past in manifold ways and in divers manners to the Fathers by the prophets,
Alfd	God, having in many sayings and in divers manners spoken in time past unto the fathers by the prophets, []
Bows	God who in several portions and in different manners in ancient times spoke to the fathers in the prophets,
ABU	God, who in many parts and in many ways spoke of old to the fathers by the prophets,
ROT(NT)	God having, **in many parts and in many ways of old**, spoken to the fathers in the prophets, —
Davi	God, having in many parts and in many ways spoken of old unto the fathers in the prophets,
RV	God, having of old time spoken unto the fathers in the prophets by divers portions and in divers manners,
Hans	God, having anciently spoken to the fathers by the prophets in many portions and in many ways,
JND	God having spoken in many parts and in many ways formerly to the fathers in the prophets,

Joyn	God, who at sundry times and in divers manners spoke in time past unto the fathers by the prophets, []
Murd	In many ways, and in many forms, God anciently conversed with our fathers, by the prophets:
Week	God, who spoke anciently in many portions and in many ways to our fathers by the prophets,
YOU	In many parts, and many ways, God of old having spoken to the fathers in the prophets,
Moff	After speaking to the fathers long ago by fragments and forms manifold in the prophets,
Twen	God, who in the old days spoke to our ancestors, through the Prophets, at many different times and in many different ways,
FEN	God, having of old spoken to our forefathers in many portions and many forms, by the prophets,
Lloy	God, having spoken in the prophets in time past, in many portions and in many ways, to the fathers,
Godb	On many occasions and in many ways in the olden time, God having spoken to the fathers through the prophets,
fBal	[] In former times it was only partially, [] And in many different ways, [] God spoke to our forefathers [] In those through whom he revealed himself. []
Weym	God, who in ancient days spoke to our forefathers in many distinct messages and by various methods through the Prophets,
ROT(B)	Whereas ⟨‖in many parts and in many ways of old‖ / God spake unto the fathers ｜ in the prophets｜⟩ /
Over	God, who at sundry times and divers manners, spake in times past unto our forefathers through the prophets,
Robe	God, who of old spoke to our forefathers in many fragments and by various methods through the Prophets,
Cunn	God, having in time past spoken to the fathers in the prophets in many portions and in many ways,
Wade	It was in many fragmentary portions and by many varied methods that God long ago conveyed his communications to our ancestors through the Prophets;
MOF	Many were the forms and fashions in which God spoke of old to our fathers by the prophets,
GOS	It was little by little and in different ways that God spoke in old times to our forefathers through the prophets,
West	God, having spoken of old to the fathers through the prophets by many partial revelations and in various ways,
Spen	God, having spoken of old to our forefathers through the prophets, by many degrees and in many ways,
cbWi	It was bit by bit and in many different ways that God in olden times spoke to our forefathers through the prophets,
Wils	God, who in days of old spoke to the fathers in the prophets, at different stages and in various ways,

Conf   God, who at sundry times and in divers manners spoke in times
           past to the fathers by the prophets,
Ford   God, who of old spake at various times and in many ways to our
           fathers by the prophets, []
BBE   In times past the word of God came to our fathers through the
           prophets, in different parts and in different ways; []
ckWi   In old times God spoke to our fathers by the prophets in many
           different ways;
RSV   In many and various ways, God spoke of old to our fathers by
           the prophets;
KNO   In old days, God spoke to our fathers in many ways and by many
           means, through the prophets;
KlLi   In many fragmentary and various utterances, God spoke of old
           to our ancestors through the prophets;
Sch1/2   At varying/various intervals/times and in varied fashions God
           spoke of old to our fathers by the prophets;
LAM   From of old God spoke to our fathers by the prophets in every
           manner and in all ways;
jbP1   God, who gave to our forefathers many different glimpses of the
           truth in the words of the prophets,
Noli   God spoke to our forefathers in old times through the Prophets
           in many places and in various ways.
Norl   In days of old, God spoke at different times and in different ways
           to our fathers, through the prophets.
Wues   In many parts and in different ways God in former times having
           spoken to the fathers by means of the prophets,
NWT   God, who long ago spoke on many occasions and in many ways
           to our forefathers by means of the prophets,
BEC   Long ago God spoke to our fathers in many different ways by the
           prophets,
AMP   In many separate revelations—each of which set forth a portion
           of the Truth—and in different ways God spoke of old to [our]
           forefathers in *and* by the prophets.[]
JB   At various times in the past and in various different ways, God
           spoke to our ancestors through the prophets;
Conc   By many portions and many modes, of old, God, speaking to the
           fathers in the prophets,
Barc   Long ago God spoke to our ancestors by means of the prophets,
           but the revelation which was given through them was fragmentary
           and varied.
Ledy   Long ago God spoke to our early fathers in many different ways.
           He spoke through the early preachers.
NBV   God of old spoke to our fathers at various times and in many
           ways by means of the prophets.
NAB1   In times past, God spoke in fragmentary and varied ways to our
           fathers through the prophets;

NEB   When in former times God spoke to our forefathers, he spoke in fragmentary and varied fashion through the prophets.

NAS   God, after He spoke long ago to the fathers in the prophets in many portions and in many ways, []

Cres   Long ago, God talked to our fathers through the prophets. He talked in many parts and in many ways.

LBP   Long ago God spoke in many different ways to our fathers through the prophets [in visions, dreams, and even face to face], telling them little by little about his plans. []

jbP2   God, who gave to our forefathers many different glimpses of the truth in the words of the prophets,

BLE   Fragmentarily and variously did God of old speak to the fathers in the prophets,

Tran   In the past God spoke to our forefathers by the prophets in many and various ways.

GNB   In the past, God spoke to our ancestors many times and in many ways through the prophets,

NIV   In the past God spoke to our forefathers through the prophets at many times and in various ways,

Simp   Long ago, God used the prophets to speak to our ancestors many times and in many ways;

Latt   God, who in ancient time spoke to our fathers in many and various ways through the prophets,

RAV   God, who at various times and in different ways spoke in time past to the fathers by the prophets, []

NJB   At many moments in the past and by many means, God spoke to our ancestors through the prophets;

NAB2   In times past, God spoke in partial and various ways to our fathers through the prophets;

KJ2   In many times and in many ways of old, God spoke to the fathers in the prophets;

ETR   In the past God spoke to our people through the prophets. God spoke to them many times and in many different ways.

TEB   In the past God spoke to our ancestors through the prophets. He spoke to them many times and in many different ways.

NRS   Long ago God spoke to our ancestors in many and various ways by the prophets,

REB   When in times past God spoke to our forefathers, he spoke in many and varied ways through the prophets.

Cass   God having spoken, in times of old, to our forefathers by the mouth of the prophets—and that on many an occasion and in many different ways —

Ster   In days gone by, God spoke in many and varied ways to the Fathers through the prophets.

CEV   Long ago in many ways and at many times God's prophets spoke his message to our ancestors.

CCB   God has spoken in the past to our fathers through the prophets,
             in many different ways, although never completely;

Table 2   Hebrews 1:2

GRK   **ep'eskhatou tōn hēmerōn toutōn elalēsen hēmin en huioi, hon
                 ethēken klēronomon pantōn, di'hou kai epoiēsen tous aiōnas;**

k.i.t.   *upon last[part] of-the days these he-spoke to-us in Son, whom
                 he-put heir of-all(things) through-whom also he-made the ages;*

WYC1   at the laste in thes dayes spac to vs in the sone whom he
                 ordeynyde ayre of alle thingis; by whom he made & the worldis.

WYC2   at the laste in these daies he hath spoke to vs bi the sone; whom
                 he hath ordeyned air of alle thingis, and bi whom he made the
                 worldis.

TYN   but in these last dayes he hath spoken vnto vs by hys sonne,
                 whom he hath made heyre of all thynges: by whom also he made
                 the worlde.

COV   but in these last dayes he hath spoken vnto vs by his sonne,
                 whom he hath made heyre of all thinges, by whom also he made
                 the worlde.

GRT   but in these last dayes he hath spoken vnto vs by hys awne
                 sonne, whom he hath made heyre of all thinges by whom also
                 he made the worlde.

GEN   in these last dayes hee hath spoken vnto vs by his Sonne, []
                 Whome hee hath made heire of all things, by whom also he made
                 the worlds, []

BIS   hath in these last dayes spoken unto us in the sonne, whom he
                 hath appoynted heire of al thynges, by whom also he made the
                 worldes. []

DOU   last of al in these daies hath spoken to vs in his Sonne, whom he
                 hath appointed heire of al, by whom he made also the worldes.

KJV*   Hath in these last dayes spoken unto us by *his* Sonne, whom he
                 hath appointed heire of all things, by whom also he made the
                 worlds; []

Whis   Hath in these last days spoken unto us by *his* Son, whom he
                 hath appointed heir of all things, by whom also he made the
                 ages.

PUR   In these last Days has spoken to us by the Son, whom he put the
                 Heir of all Things, by whom also he made the Worlds. []

Wynn   hath, in these last days, spoken to us by the SON, whom he
                 constituted heir of all things, by whom He also made the worlds;

Harw   hath now in this last of his dispensations spoken to us by his
                 Son, [] whom he hath constituted universal governor, and by
                 whom he arranged the order of his various dispensations. []

Wors   hath in these last days spoken to us by *his* Son, whom He hath
                 appointed heir of all *things*, by whom also He made the worlds.

CHA   last of all, in these days hath spoken to us by his Son, whom he hath appointed heir of all things, by whom also he made the world.

Wesl   hath in these last days spoken to us by *his* Son; Whom he hath appointed heir of all things, by whom he also made the worlds:

Hawe   in these last days hath spoken to us by *s* Son, whom he hath appointed heir of all things, by whom also he made the worlds;

Newc   in these last days hath spoken to Us by *his* Son, whom he hath appointed heir of all things, by whom he made the worlds also:

Scar   hath, in these last days, spoken to us by *his* SON; whom he hath appointed heir of all *things*, by whom he also constituted the ages:

THO   hath in these last days spoken to us by a son whom he hath constituted heir of all things, by whom also he made the ages;

Will   has, in these last Days, accosted us, through his Son, Whom He has appointed an Heir of the Whole; through Whom indeed He formed the Worlds:

RAE   Hath in these last days spoken unto us by his Son, whom he hath appointed heir (and possessor) of all things, by whom also he made the worlds;

Thom   Hath in these last days spoken to us by his Son, whom he appointed heir of all things, through whom he also made the worlds; []

Dodd   —Hath in these last days spoken to us by his son, whom he constituted heir of all things; through whom also he made the worlds,

Bels   in the last of these days hath spoken to Us by *his* Son, whom he hath appointed heir of all things, for whom also he constituted the ages:

Dick   has in these last periods communicated to us by a Son, whom he has constituted proprietor of all things, through whom also he made the worlds;

Penn   at the end of those days spake to us by *his* Son, whom he hath appointed heir of all things, by whom also he made the worlds; []

Camp   has in these last days spoken to us by a Son, whom he has constituted Lord of all things, by whom also he made the universe;

Tayl   hath in these last days spoken unto us by His Son, whom he hath appointed heir of all things, by whom also he made the worlds;

Hein   Hath in these last days spoken unto us by a son, whom he appointed heir of all men, with respect to which even he made the past Dispensations of man; []

BOO   But in these last days he hath spoken to us by his Son, whom he hath appointed heir of all things, by whom also he made the worlds,

SHA	hath at the last of these days spoken to us by a Son, whom he hath appointed heir of all things, by whom also he made the ages.
Sawy	in these last days spoke to us by his Son, whom he appointed heir of all things, through whom also he made the worlds,
High	Hath in these last days spoken unto us by his Son, whom he appointed heir of all things, by whom also he made the worlds; []
Ains	hath at the end of these days spoken to us by *his* Son, Whom he appointed heir of all things, by whom also he made the ages.
Alfd	At the end of these days spake unto us in his Son, whom he appointed heir of all things, by whom he also made the worlds; []
Bows	At the end of these days spake unto us in *his* Son, whom he constituted heir of all things, through whom also he made the ages;
ABU	in these last days spoke to us by his Son, whom he appointed heir of all things, by whom he also made the worlds;
ROT(NT)	—**at a last stage of these days** spoke to us in a Son; whom he appointed Heir of all things, through whom also he made the ages;
Davi	at the end of these days spake to us in the Son, whom he appointed heir of all things, through whom also he made the worlds;
RV	hath at the end of these days spoken unto us in *his* Son, whom he appointed heir of all things, through whom also he made the worlds;
Hans	has in [the] last of these days spoken to us by a son, whom he appointed heir of all things, through whom, also, he prepared the aeons;
JND	at the end of these days has spoken to us in [the person of the] Son, whom he has established heir of all things, by whom also he made the worlds;
Joyn	Hath in these last days spoken unto us by the Son of man, whom he hath appointed heir of all things, by whom also he made the worlds; []
Murd	But in these latter days, he hath conversed with us, by his Son; whom he hath constituted heir of all things, and by whom he made the worlds;
Week	hath in these later days spoken to us by a Son, whom he appointed heir of all things, and through whom he made the universe;
YOU	in these last days did speak to us in a Son, whom He appointed heir of all things, through whom also He did make the ages;
Moff	God spoke to us at the end of these days in a Son, whom he appointed heir of all things, through whom also he made the worlds;
Twen	has in these latter days spoken to us through the Son, whom he

had appointed heir to everything, and through whom he had made the universe.

ROT(B) | At the end of these days| / He hath spoken unto us in | his Son|,— / Whom he hath appointed heir of all things, / Through whom also he hath made the ages; /

FEN at last in these times has spoken to us by a Son: Whom He appointed Inheritor of all; and through Whom He made the ages;

Lloy Hath at the end of these days spoken to us by a Son, whom He hath appointed heir of all things; through whom also He made the worlds;

Godb at the last of these days has spoken to us through his Son, whom he put forth the heir of all things, and through whom he created the ages;

fBal [] But in these last days he has once for all spoken to us [] In his Son, [] Whom he appointed heir of everything, [] And through whom he made the worlds. [][]

Over hath in these latter days spoken unto us through a Son, whom He appointed an heir of all things; and for whom also He created the universe;

Robe has at the end of these days spoken to us through a Son, who is the predestined Lord of the universe, and through whom He made the world.

Cunn hath at the end of these days apoken to us in a Son, whom he appointed heir of all things; through whom also he made the worlds;

Wade but at the end of the present period of history He has communicated with us through One Who is a Son—a Son Whom He has constituted heir of all things; for through Him He also made the world, with its successive Ages.

Mof but in these days at the end he has spoken to us by a Son—a Son whom he has appointed heir of the universe, as it was by him that he created the world.

GOS but in these latter days he has spoken to us in a Son, whom he had destined to possess everything, and through whom he had made the world.

West in these last days hath spoken to us by one who is Son, whom he hath set up as the heir of all things; by whom also he created the ages.

Spen has at last in these days spoken to us by His SON, whom He appointed Heir of all things, and through whom He made the worlds.

cbWi but in these latter days He has spoken to us through a Son, whom He had appointed lawful owner of everything, and through whom He had made the worlds.

Wils has at the end of these days spoken to us in the Son, whom He appointed heir of all things, through whom also He made the worlds;

Conf   last of all in these days has spoken to us by his Son, whom he appointed heir of all things, by whom also he made the world;

Ford   Has in these last days spoken to us by his Son, whom he has appointed heir of all things, by whom also he made the worlds; []

BBE   But now, at the end of these days, it has come to us through his Son, to whom he has given all things for a heritage, and through whom he made the order of the generations; []

ckWi   in these last days he has spoken to us by a Son; he appointed him the heir of all the world; he created the world through him;

RSV   but in these last days he has spoken to us by a Son, whom he appointed the heir of all things, through whom also he created the world.

KNO   now at last in these times he has spoken to us, with a Son to speak for him; a Son, whom he has appointed to inherit all things, just as it was through him that be created this world of time;

KlLi   at the present time, the final epoch, he has spoken to us through his Son, whom he has appointed heir of the universe. Through him, too, he made the world.

Sch1/2 but at the close of these times he has spoken to us by a Son, whom he appointed heir to everything. By him also he instituted the Aeons.

LAM   and in these latter days he has spoken to us by his Son.[] Whom he has appointed heir of all things, and by whom also he made the worlds; []

Noli   In these latter days he has spoken to us through his Son, whom he appointed heir of the universe and through whom he created the world.

Norl   Now at last, in these days, God has been speaking to us through His Son! And He has been given everything for a heritage, even as it was through Him that the universe was created.

Wues   in the last of these days spoke to us in One who by nature is [His] Son, whom He appointed heir of all things, through whom also He constituted the ages;

NWT   has at the end of these days spoken to us by means of a Son, whom he appointed heir of all things, and through whom he made the systems of things.

BEC   but in these last days He has spoken to us by His Son, whom He made the heir of everything and by whom He made the world.

AMP   [But] in the last of these days He has spoken to us in [the person of a] Son, Whom He appointed Heir *and* lawful Owner of all things, also by *and* through Whom He created the worlds *and* the reaches of space *and* the ages of time—[that is,] He made, produced, built, operated and arranged them in order. []

JB   but in our own time, the last days, he has spoken to us through
            his Son, the Son that he has appointed to inherit everything and
            through whom he made everything there is.

Conc   in the last of these days speaks to us in a Son, Whom He appoints
            enjoyer of the allotment of all, through Whom He also makes the
            eons;

Barc   But now, as time as we know it is coming to an end, he has
            spoken in one whose relation to himself is that of Son, that Son
            into whose possession he gave all things, and by whose agency
            he created the present world and the world to come.

Ledy   But in these last days He has spoken to us through His Son. God
            gave His Son everything. It was by His Son that God made the
            world.

NBV   But He has at the end of these days spoken to us in His Son,
            whom He has appointed Heir of all things and through whom
            He made the world.

NAB1   in this, the final age, he has spoken to us through his Son, whom
            he has made heir of all things and through whom he first created
            the universe.

NEB   But in this the final age he has spoken to us in the Son whom
            he has made heir to the whole universe, and through whom he
            created all orders of existence:

NAS   in these last days has spoken to us in *His* Son, whom He
            appointed heir of all things, through whom also He made the
            world. []

Cres   In these last days, he talked to us through his Son. God chose
            him to be the one to whom he would give all things. God also
            made the world by this Son.

LBP   But now in these days he has spoken to us through his Son to
            whom he has given everything, and through whom he made the
            world and everything there is. []

jbP2   has now, at the end of the present age, given us the truth in the
            Son. Through the Son God made the whole universe, and to the
            Son he has ordained that all creation shall ultimately belong.

BLE   but has in these latter days spoken to us in a Son whom he has
            appointed heir to everything, through whom also he made the
            universe;

Tran   Now at the end of this age he has spoken to us by a Son. It was
            through him that God made the universe, and he has appointed
            him to enter into possession of the whole world.

GNB   but in these last days he has spoken to us through his Son. He
            is the one through whom God created the universe, the one
            whom God has chosen to possess all things at the end.

NIV   but in these last days he has spoken to us by his Son, whom he
            appointed heir of all things, and through whom he made the
            universe.

Simp   but, during these last times, God used *His* Son to speak to us.
            God appointed him to inherit everything. Through him God
            made the universe.

RAV   has in these last days spoken to us by *his* Son, whom he has
            appointed heir of all things, through whom also he made the
            worlds; []

Latt   has now in these last days spoken to us through his son, whom
            he made the heir to all things and through whom he also created
            the ages.

NJB   but in our time, the final days, he has spoken to us in the person
            of his Son, whom he appointed heir of all things and through
            whom he made the ages.

NAB2   in these last days, he spoke to us through a son, whom he made
            heir of all things and through whom he created the universe,

KJ2   in these last days *He* spoke to us in *the* Son, whom He appointed
            heir of all; through whom He indeed made the ages;

ETR   And now in these last days God has spoken to us again. God has
            spoken to us through his Son. God made the whole world
            through his Son. And God has chosen his Son to have all things.

TEB   And now in these last days God has spoken to us through his
            Son. God has chosen his Son to own all things. And he made
            the world through the Son.

NRS   but in these last days he has spoken to us by a Son, whom he
            appointed heir of all things, through whom he also created the
            worlds.

REB   But in this the final age he has spoken to us in his Son, whom
            he has appointed heir of all things; and through him he created
            the universe.

Cass   has now, at the close of these days of ours, spoken to us in the
            person of one who is his Son, whom he has appointed to possess
            all things as his inheritance, just as it was through him that he
            created whatever there has been throughout the ages

Ster   But now, in the *acharit-hayamim*, he has spoken to us through
            his Son, to whom he has given ownership of everything and
            through whom he created the universe.

CEV   But now at last God sent his Son to bring his message to us. God
            created the universe by his Son, and everything will someday
            belong to the Son.

CCB   but in our times he has spoken definitively to us through his
            Son.[] He is the one God appointed heir of all things, since
            through him he unfolded the stages of the world.[]

Table 3   Hebrews 1:3a

**GRK   hos ōn apaugasma tēs doxēs kai kharaktēr tes hypostaseōs
           autou, pherōn te ta panta toi rhēmati tēs dynameōs autou,**

k.i.t.	who being beaming-forth-from of-the glory and impress of-the sub-standing of-him, bearing and the all(things) to-the saying of-the power of-him,
WYC1	The whiche whanne he is the schynynge of glorie & fygure of his substaunce & berynge alle thingis by worde of his vertue
WYC2	Which whanne also he is the brightnesse of glorie, and figure of his substaunce, and berith alle thingis bi word of his vertu,
TYN	Which sonne beynge the brightnes of his glory, and very ymage off his substance, bearynge vppe all thynges with the worde of his power,
COV	Which (sonne) beynge the brightnes of his glory, & the very ymage of his substaunce, bearinge vp all thinges with the worde of his power,
GRT	Whych (sonne) beinge the brightnes of hys glory, and the very ymage of hys substance rulynge all thynges wyth the worde of hys power,
GEN	Who being the brightnes of the glory, and ingraued forme of his person, & bearing vp all things by his mighty word,
BIS	Who beyng the brightnesse of the glory, & the very image of his substance, upholding al thinges with the woord of his power,
DOU	Who being the brightnesse of his glorie and the figure of his substance, and carying all things by the word of his power,
KJV*	Who being the brightnesse of his glory, and the expresse image of his person, and upholding all things by the word of his power,
Whis	Who being a beam of his glory, and the express image of his substance, and upholding all things by the word of his power,
PUR	Who being the Brightness of the Glory, the Mark of his Substance, and supporting all Things with his powerful Word;
Wynn	who, being the effulgence of his glory, and the express image of his person, and upholding all things by the word of his power,
Harw	This most illustrious Personage, who was a radiant beam emitted from the supreme glory, the fair impression of the essential form of the divinity, and who is now invested with the universal administration of all things,
Wors	Who being the refulgence of his glory and the imprest image of his person, and sustaining all things by his powerful word,
CHA	Who being the brightness of his glory, and the figure of his substance, and upholding all things by the word of his power,
Wesl	Who being the brightness of his glory, and the express image of his person, and sustaining all things by the word of his power,
Hawe	who being the splendour of his glory, and the very impress of his substance, and upholding all things with his powerful word,
Newc	who, being the brightness of his glory, and the express image of his person, and ruling all things by his powerful word,
Scar	who, being the effulgence of his glory, and express image of his substance, and sustaining all things by the word of his power,

THO	who being an effulgence of the glory, and an impress of his substance, and upholding all things by the word of his power,
Will	who being the *Effulgence* of his Glory, and the *Representative* of his *Subsistence*, and supporting the Universe by the Mandate of his Power,
RAE	Who, being the brightness of his glory, and the express impression of his person, and upholding the universe by the word of his power,
Thom	Who being the effulgence of his glory, and the express image of his substance, and upholding all things by the word of his power,
Dodd	Who, being an effulgence of his glory, and an exact image of his substance, and upholding all things by the word of his power,
Bels	who, being a ray of *his* brightness, and an image of his perfections, and ruling all things by his powerful word,
Dick	who, (being an effulgence of his glory, and an accurate representation of his existence, and sustaining all things by his own powerful word),
Penn	who being the effulgence of *his* glory, and the impression of his substance, and making all things manifest by the word of his power,
Camp	who, being an effulgence of his glory and an exact representation of his character, and controlling all things by his own powerful word,
Tayl	who (being *the* brightness of *his* glory, and *the* image of his substance, and upholding all things by the word of his power,)
Hein	who being an effulgence of his glory, and an express image of his consistency, even sustaining everything contained in the promise concerning his power,
BOO	Who being the brightness of his glory, and the express image of his substance, and upholding all things by his powerful word,
SHA	Who being a ray of his glory and an image of his substance, and upholding all things by the word of his power,
Sawy	who being the brightness of his glory and the express image of his substance, and sustaining all things by the word of his power,
High	Who being the brightness of his glory, and the express image of his person, and upholding all things, by the word of his power,
Ains	Who being the brightness of his glory, and the exact resemblance of him, and upholding all things by the word of his power,
Alfd	Who being the brightness of his glory and the express image of his substance, and upholding the universe by the word of his power,
Bows	Who being the radiance of *his* glory and the express image of his essential nature, and upholding all things by the word of his power,

ABU　　　who, being the brightness of his glory and the impress of his substance, and upholding all things by the word of his power,

ROT(NT)　who, —being an eradiated brightness of [his] glory and an exact expression of his essence, also bearing up all things by the declaration of his power,

Davi　　who being an effulgence of the glory and express image of his substance, and bearing all things by the word of his power,

RV　　　who being the effulgence of his glory, and the very image of his substance, and upholding all things by the word of his power,

Hans　　who, being a beam of his glory, and an impress of his substance, and sustaining all things by the word of his power,

JND　　　who being [the] effulgence of his glory and [the] expression of his substance, and upholding all things by the word of his power,

Joyn　　who being the brightness of his glory, and the express image of his person, and upholding all things by the word of his power,

Murd　　who is the splendour of his glory, and the image of himself, and upholdeth all by the energy of his word;

Week　　who, being a shining forth of the brightness of his glory, and a portrait of his nature, and bearing up all things by the word of his power,

YOU　　who being the brightness of the glory, and the impress of His subsistence, bearing up also the all things by the saying of his might —

Moff　　who, as the reflected radiance of his majesty and the *facsimile* of his nature, sustaining also all things with the word of his power,

Twen　　He is the reflection of God's Glory and the embodiment of the divine nature, and upholds all creation by the power of his word.

ROT(B)　Who ᵉbeing an eradiated brightness of his glory, / And an exact representation of his very being, / Also bearing up all things by the utterance of his power, /

FEN　　Who—being the effulgence of His grandeur, and the representative of His essence, supporting all things by His powerful decree —

Lloy　　who, being the effulgence of His glory, and the very image of His Being, and upholding all things by the word of his power,

Godb　　who being the brightness of his glory, and the character of his person, and holding up all things by the word of his power,

fBal　　[]He is the reflected perfection of God, [] And the imprint of the divine nature. [] And it is he who sustains everything [] By the expression of his power. []

Over　　who, being a radiant reflection of His glory, and a complete expression of His being, and upholding all spiritual creation by the power of his word,

Robe　　He brightly reflects God's glory and is the exact representation

	of His being, and upholds the universe by His all-powerful word.
Cunn	who being the effulgence of his glory and the impress of his essence, and upholding all things by the word of his power,
Wade	He, being the Radiance of God's Glory and the Imprint of His Reality (*reproducing it as truly as the seal reproduces the signet*) and sustaining the Universe by the expression of His mighty Will,
MOF	He, reflecting God's bright glory and stamped with God's own character, sustains the universe with his word of power;
GOS	He is the reflection of God's glory, and the representation of his being, and bears up the universe by his mighty word.
West	He, being the flashing-forth of his glory, and the very expression of his being, sustaineth all things by God's word of power;
Spen	He being the effulgence of God's glory and the very image of His substance, upholding the universe by God's powerful mandate. []
cbWi	He is the reflection of God's glory and the perfect representation of His being, and continues to uphold the universe by His mighty word.
Wils	who being the radiance of His glory, and the very image of His Being, and upholding all things by the word of His power,
Conf	who, being the brightness of his glory and the image of his substance, and upholding all things by the word of his power,
Ford	Who being the brightness of his glory, and the very impress of his substance, and upholding all things by the word of his power,
BBE	Who, being the outshining of his glory, the true image of his substance, supporting all things by the word of his power,
ckWi	he is the reflection of God's glory and the living image of his being; he holds up the world by his word of power;
RSV	He reflects the glory of God and bears the very stamp of his nature, upholding the universe by his word of power.
KNO	a Son, who is the radiance of his Father's splendour, and the full expression of his being; all creation depends, for its support, on his enabling word.
KlLi	This Son is the radiant reflection of God's glory, and the express image of his nature, conserving all things by his mighty command.
Sch1/2	He, being the reflection of God's glory and the exact expression of his nature, bringing everything into being by the exercise of God's power,
LAM	For he is the brightness of his glory and the express image of his being, upholding all things by the power of his word;
Noli	He is the reflection of the divine glory and substance. He upholds all creation through the powerful mandate of God.
Norl	He is the radiance of God's glory, and the exact image of God's nature. He upholds all creation by His almighty Word.

Wues	who, being the out-raying (effulgence) of His glory and the exact reproduction of His essence, and sustaining, guiding, and propelling all things by the word of His power,
NWT	He is the reflection of [his] glory and the exact representation of his very being, and he sustains all things by the word of his power;
BEC	He who shines with God's glory and is the copy of His being carries everything by His mighty Word
AMP	He is the sole expression of the glory of God—the Light-being, the out-raying of the divine—and He is the perfect imprint and very image of [God's] nature, upholding and maintaining and guiding and propelling the universe by His mighty word of power.
JB	He is the radiant light of God's glory and the perfect copy of his nature, sustaining the universe by his powerful command;
Conc	Who, being the Effulgence of His glory and Emblem of His assumption, besides carrying on all by His powerful declaration,
Barc	This Son is the radiance of his glory, just as the ray is the light of the sun. He is the exact impression of his being, just as the mark is the exact impression of the seal. It is he who sustains all things by the dynamic power of his word.
Ledy	The Son shines with the shining greatness of the Father. The Son is as God is in every way. It is the Son Who holds up the whole world by the power of His Word.
NBV	As the reflection of God's glory and the true expression of His being He sustains the universe by His almighty word.
NAB1	This Son is the reflection of the Father's glory, the exact representation of the Father's being, and he sustains all things by his powerful word.
NEB	the Son who is the effulgence of God's splendour and the stamp of God's very being, and sustains the universe by his word of power.
NAS	And He is the radiance of His glory and the exact representation of His nature, and upholds all things by the word of His power.
Cres	He shines as bright as God. He is just like God himself. He holds up the world by the power of his word.
LBP	God's Son shines out with God's glory, and all that God's Son is and does marks him as God. He regulates the universe by the mighty power of his command.
jbP1/2	This Son, radiance of the glory of God, flawless expression of the nature of God, himself the upholding principle / power of all thst is,
BLE	who being beam of his glory and imprint of his essence, and actuating all things by his word of power,
Tran	He radiates God's glory, he shows us exactly what God's nature is, and by his powerful word he upholds the universe.

GNB   He reflects the brightness of God's glory and is the exact likeness of God's own being, sustaining the universe with his powerful word.

NIV   The Son is the radiance of God's glory and the exact representation of his being, sustaining all things by his powerful word.

Simp The Son is the shining brightness of God's glory and the exact picture of God's real being. The Son holds up the universe with his powerful word.

KJ2   who being the shining splendor of His glory, and the express image of His essence, and upholding all things by the word of His power,

RAV   who being the brightness of his glory and the express image of his person, and upholding all things by the word of his power,

Latt He is the gleam of his glory and the representation of his nature, he carries all things by his word of power;

NJB   He is the reflection of God's glory and bears the impress of God's own being, sustaining all things by his powerful command;

NAB2 who is the refulgence of his glory,/ the very imprint of his being,/ and who sustains all things by his mighty word./

ETR   The Son shows the glory of God. He is a perfect copy of God's nature. The Son holds everything together with his powerful command.

TEB   The Son reflects the glory of God. He is an exact copy of God's nature. He holds everything together with his powerful word.

NRS   He is the reflection of God's glory and the exact imprint of God's very being, and he sustains all things by his powerful word.

REB   He is the radiance of God's glory, the stamp of God's very being, and he sustains the universe by his word of power.

Cass It is he who radiates forth God's glory, who is the precise counterpart of his very being, who sustains all things by his mighty word of command.

Ster This Son is the radiance of the Sh'khinah, the very expression of God's essence, upholding all that exists by his powerful word;

CEV   God's Son has all the brightness of God's own glory and is like him in every way. By his own mighty word he holds the universe together. []

CCB   He is the radiance of God's Glory and bears the stamp of God's hidden being, so that his powerful word upholds the universe.

Table 4   Hebrews 1:3b

GRK   **katharismon tōn hamartiōn poiēsamenos ekathisen en dexiai tēs megalosynēs en hupsēlois,**

k.i.t. *cleansing of-the sins having-made he-sat-down on right(hand) of-the greatness in lofty(places)*

WYC1	makyng purgacon of synnes; sittith on the righthalfe of mageste in highe thingis []
WYC2	he makith purgacioun of synnes, and syttith on the righthalf of the maieste in heuenes;
TYN	hath in his awne persone pourged oure synnes, and is sytten on the right honde of the maiestie an hye,
COV	hath in his owne personne pourged oure synnes, and is set on the right hande of the maiestie on hye:
GRT	hath by his awne person pourged oure synnes, and sytteth on the right hande of the maiestye on hye
GEN	hath by himselfe purged our sinnes, and sitteth at the right hand of the maiestie in the highest places, []
BIS	having by him selfe purged our sinnes, hath sit on the right hand of the maiestie on high :[]
DOU	making purgation of sinnes, sitteth on the right hand of the Maiestie in the high places:
KJV*	when hee had by himselfe purged our sinnes, sate down on ye right hand of the Maiestie on high; []
Whis	when he had by himself purged our sins, sat down on the right hand of the Majesty on high:
PUR	when he had made a Cleansing of our Sins by himself, sate down at the right Hand of the Majesty on high: []
Wynn	when he had by himself effected the cleansing of our sins, sat down on the right-hand of the Majesty on high;
Harw	after he had totally expunged our crimes, was gloriously advanced to the most exalted dignity at the right hand of the eternal Majesty:
Wors	having by himself performed the purging away of our sins, sat down at the right hand of the majesty on high.
CHA	making purgation of sins, sitteth on the right hand of the majesty on high,
Wesl	when he had by himself purged our sins, sat down on the right hand of the Majesty on high:
Hawe	by himself having effected the cleansing of our sins, he sat down at the right hand of Majesty on high;
Newc	when had made a cleansing of [our] sins, by *the sacrifice of* himself, sat down on the right hand of the *divine* Majesty on high;
Scar	having by himself effected the purification of our sins, sat down on the right hand of the Majesty on high:
THO	having by himself made a purification of our sins, sat down on the right hand of the majesty on high,
Will	having effected the Purification of our Sins through Himself, became seated at the Right Hand of the Majesty on High.
RAE	when he had by himself purged away our sins, sat down on the right hand of the Majesty on high;

Thom	when he had by himself procured the expurgation of our sins, sat down on the right hand of the majesty amid high beings; []
Dodd	when he had made purification of our sins by himself, sat down at the right hand of the majesty in high places.
Bels	when he had by himself made a cleansing of [our] sins, sat down on the right hand of the Majesty on high;
Dick	when he had by himself accomplished a purification for our sins, sat down at the right hand of the Majesty in the highest heavens,
Penn	when he had accomplished the purifying of sins, sat down on the right hand of the Majesty on high; []
Tayl	after he had by himself made purification of our sins, sat down at the right hand of the Majesty on high;
Camp	after he had by himself made expiation for our sins sat down at the right hand of the Majesty on high;
Hein	having of himself effected an expiation for our sins, sat down on the right hand of the Majesty on high. []
BOO	when he had by himself made expiation for our sins, sat down on the right hand of the Majesty on high:
SHA	when he had by himself made a cleansing of our sins, sat down on the right hand of the Majesty on high;
Sawy	having made a purification of sins, sat down on the right hand of the majesty on high,
High	when he had by himself purged our sins, sat down on the right hand of the Majesty on high; []
Ains	having made a purification of sins, sat down on the right hand of the Majesty on high;
Alfd	when he had made purification of sins, sat down on the right hand of majesty on high; []
Bows	when he had made a purification from sins, sat down at the right hand of the majesty on high,
ABU	when he had by himself made a cleansing of sins, sat down on the right hand of the Majesty on high;
ROT(NT)	having achieved a **purification of [our] sins**,—sat down on [the] right hand of the majesty in high [places];
Davi	having made purification of sins, sat down at the right hand of the Majesty on high;
RV	when he had made purification of sins, sat down on the right hand of the Majesty on high;
Hans	when he had made purification of sins, sat down at [the] right hand of [the] Majesty in high places;
JND	having made [by himself] the purification of sins, set himself down on the right hand of the greatness on high,
Joyn	when he had made a purification from sins, sat down on the right hand of the majesty on high; []

Murd	and by himself he made purgation of sins, and sat down on the right hand of the Majesty on high.
Week	when he had himself prepared a cleansing from sin, sat down on the right hand of the Majesty on High,
YOU	through himself having made a cleansing of our sins, sat down at the right hand of the greatness in the highest,
Moff	*sat down*, after he had made purification of sins, *at the right hand* of the Sovereignty on high,
Twen	He made an expiation for the sins of men, and then *took his seat at the right hand* of God's Majesty on high,
ROT(B)	|Purification of sins| having achieved› / SAT DOWN ON THE RIGHT HAND of the majesty in high places: /
FEN	having made a purification from sins, seated Himself in right of the Majesty on high;
Lloy	when he had [hy himself] made purification of sins, sat down at the right hand of the Majesty on high;
Godb	having made purgation of the sins, sat down on the right hand of the Majesty on high;
fBal	[] So when he had cleared men from the guilt of sin, [] He sat down on the right of the Majesty on high. []
Over	having exemplified the possible demonstration of the nullification of evil on our behalf, sat down on the right hand of the majesty of God on high,
Robe	After securing man's purification from sin He took His seat at the right hand of the Majesty on high,
Cunn	after making a cleansing from sins took his seat at the right hand of the Majesty on high,
Wade	after having secured for us purification from our sins, took His seat at the right hand of the Majesty on high,
Mof	when he had secured our purification from sins, he sat down at the right hand of the Majesty on high;
GOS	He has effected man's purification from sin, and has taken his seat on high at the right hand of God's Majesty,
West	and having made a cleansing from sin, 'hath taken his seat at the right hand' of Majesty on high,
Spen	After effecting purification from sins, HE SEATED HIMSELF AT THE RIGHT HAND of the Majesty on high,
cbWi	After He had procured man's purification from sins, He took His seat at the right hand of God's majesty,
Wils	when he had made atonement for sins, sat down at the right hand of the Majesty on high,
Conf	has effected man's purgation from sin and taken his seat at the right hand of the Majesty on high,
Ford	when he had by himself made purification of our sins, sat down at the right hand of the Majesty on high; []

BBE	having given himself as an offering making clean from sins, took his seat at the right hand of God in heaven; []
ckWi	when he had made purification from sin, he took his seat at the right hand of the majesty on high;
RSV	When he had made purification for sins, he sat down at the right hand of the Majesty on high,
KNO	Now, making atonement for our sins, he has taken his place on high, at the right hand of God's majesty,
KlLi	After he had cleansed us from sin, he took his seat at the right hand of the Majesty on high,
Sch1/2	when he had effected an expiation for sins, sat down at the right hand of the Majesty in the heavenly heights.
LAM	and when he had through his person cleansed our sins, then he sat down on the right hand of the Majesty on high;[]
jbP1	effected in person the reconciliation between God and man and then took his seat at the right hand of the majesty on high—
Noli	He has cleansed man from sin. He sits at the right hand of God in heaven. []
Norl	He himself made atonement for our sins, and then sat down on the right hand of God the Father on high.[]
Wues	having made purification of sins, sat down on the right hand of the Majesty on high;
NWT	and after he had made a purification for our sins he sat down on the right hand of the Majesty in lofty places.
BEC	He made a cleansing from sins, *sat down at the right* of the Majesty in heaven,
AMP	When He had by offering Himself accomplished *our cleansing of sins and riddance of guilt,* He sat down at the right hand of the divine Majesty on high, []
JB	and now that he has destroyed the defilement of sin, he has gone to take his place in heaven at the right hand of divine Majesty,
Conc	making a cleansing of sins, is seated at the right hand of the Majesty in the heights;
Barc	And, after he had effected the cleansing of men from their sins, he took his place at the right hand of the Majesty in the heights of heaven;
Ledy	The Son gave his own life so we could be clean from all sin. After He had done that, He sat down on the right side of God in heaven.
NBV	And when He has effected our cleansing from sin, He took His seat at the right hand of the Majesty on high.
NEB	When he had brought about the purgation of sins, he took his seat at the right hand of the Majesty on high,
NAB1	When he had cleansed us from our sins, he took his seat at the right hand of the Majesty in heaven,

Cres	He cleaned away people's bad ways. Then he sat down beside God in heaven.
LBP	He is the one who died to cleanse us and clear our record of all sin, and then sat down in highest honor beside the great God of heaven
jbP2	having effected in person the cleansing of men's sin, took his seat at the right hand of the majesty on high—
BLE	took his seat at the right hand of the Majesty on high when he had made purgation of sins,
Tran	When he had made it possible for man to be cleansed from sin, he sat down at the right hand of Almighty God in heaven,
GNB	After achieving forgiveness for the sins of mankind, he sat down in heaven at the right-hand side of God, the Supreme Power.[]
NIV	After he had provided purification for sins, he sat down at the right hand of the Majesty in heaven.
Simp	After he had provided a cleansing from sin, he sat down at God's right side in heaven.
RAV	when he had by himself purged our sins, sat down at the right hand of the Majesty on high, []
KJ2	having made purification of our sins through Himself, *He* sat down on *the* right of the Majesty on high,
Latt	and when he has caused purification from sins, he took his seat on the right hand of the majesty, in the highest;
NJB	and now that he has purged sins away, he has taken his seat at the right hand of the divine Majesty on high.
NAB2	/When he had accomplished purification from sins,/ he took his seat at the right hand of the Majesty on high,/
NAS	When He had made purification of sins, He sat down at the right hand of the Majesty on high;
ETR	The Son made people clean from their sins. Then he sat down at the right side of the Great One (*God*) in heaven.
TEB	The Son made people clean from their sins. Then he sat down at the right side of God, the Great One in heaven.
NRS	When he had made purification for sins, he sat down at the right hand of the Majesty on high,
REB	When he had brought about purification from sins, he took his seat at the right hand of God's Majesty on high,
Cass	Moreover, having accomplished the purging away of sins, **he took his seat at the right hand** of the divine Majesty on high,
Ster	and after he had, through himself, made purification for sins, he **sat down at the right hand** of *HaG'dulah BaM'romim.*[]
CEV	After the Son had washed away our sins, he sat down at the right side of the glorious God in heaven.
CCB	And after taking away sin, he took his place at the right hand of the divine Majesty in Heaven.[]

7

Close to the original form?

If you cast your eye down all the different versions displayed in the four tables of ch. 6, you would see that some versions, especially the older ones, imitate the form of the original Greek wording very closely, in some cases obscuring the meaning; while other versions seem to communicate the meaning of the original more faithfully.

7.1   CLOSE TO THE WRITTEN FORM

At the end of Galatians, Colossians, 2 Thessalonians, and Philemon, Paul explicitly refers to his writing the conclusion in his own hand as a mark of genuineness; only Stern gives us, after the normally-printed body of the letter, a visible imitation of such hand-writing, while Simple uses block capitals in Gal. 6:11, Col. 4:18, 2 Thess. 3:17, and GNB uses italics in the latter two cases and in Philemon 19. In other words, an assumed form of the original is somehow imitated in these versions.

Some of the Psalms were constructed as acrostics, that is, every line, or group of lines, begins with the successive letters of the Hebrew alphabet, for literary, and perhaps pedagogical, reasons. In some English versions, Ps. 119 is divided into stanzas which are each headed with these Hebrew letters in succession from *aleph* to *tau*. The Knox version is the only one to attempt an English acrostic for each of the relevant Psalms (25, 34, 37, 111, 112, 119, 145), Prov. 31:10–31, and Lam. 1–4; NJB does so only for Ps. 25. Provided it can be done without distorting the original meaning, this is another imitation of the original form, which could be attempted, difficult though it is.

7.2 CLOSE TO THE FORM OF NAMES AND OTHER WORDS

In 4.3 we gave Mk. 1:4 as an example of transliteration from Greek letters to English letters; and the result was said to be meaningless in English. But three of these anglicized Greek words do actually give us some meaning: *Iōannēs* and *baptizōn*, *baptisma*. The first of these is a proper name; from Mk. 1, we also find *Markon*, *Iēsou Christou*, *Esaïa*, *Ioudaia*, *Nazaret*, *Iordanē*, which are a mixture of names of people and of places.

All such proper names are likely to be transliterated from the original Hebrew or Greek forms to English as far as they can be. Some transliterations follow the original closely like those above and those found in FEN and BLE; GEN had *Izhak* and BIS *Isahac* for KJV *Isaac*. Older Catholic versions, and to some extent KJV too, tended to follow latinized versions of names like 'Jonas', 'Joses', 'Sophonias'. But the most familiar English forms are generally to be preferred: 'John', 'Mark', 'Jesus', 'Isaiah', 'Judea', 'Nazareth', 'Jordan', 'Isaac', 'Jonah', 'Joseph', 'Zephaniah', as in most modern English versions.

The pronunciation of these unfamiliar foreign names could be facilitated, both by dividing into syllables: 'El'e'a'zar' NWT, Stern; and by marking the stressed syllable: 'Elea´zar' NWT, RSV, though it would seem to be more easily understood if the acute accent appeared directly above the stressed vowel, as in Knox NT (app. I), or if the whole syllable was in bold type, as in Stern (footnotes and glossary).

In the Old Testament, the name of God was written (some 6828 times) with the Hebrew consonants for 'YHWH'. With its own vowels this is transliterated into English as *Yahweh* (ROT, NJB, CCB).

But, traditionally, Jews came to feel that the divine

name itself was too holy to be pronounced, and so it came to be read aloud with the substitute 'ǝdonay (literally, 'my Lord'). A combination of the original consonants with the vowels of the substitute produced YǝHoWaH, wrongly latinized as 'Jehovah', used in some proper names in KJV (eg. Ex. 17:15 'Jehovah Nissi' where NAS has 'The Lord is My Banner'); but as the regular name for God only in JND, YOU, ASV, BLE, KJ2, NWT. (NWT has no warrant at all for introducing that name 237 times into the New Testament as the original Greek has *Kyrios*, 'Lord'.)

One of these proper names for God, perhaps the better-known one, should be used to translate 'YHWH' throughout the OT; but most especially in Ex. 3:14–5 (NEB); 6:3 'By my name Jehovah' (KJV, NEB);1 Ki. 18:39 'Jehovah, he is God.'—which hardly even make sense without the actual name; similarly, Ex. 5:2; Gen. 31:49–50; Lev. 24:16; 2 Ki. 2:24; 5:11; Ps. 83:18 (KJV); 110:1; Ex. 34:6 (NEB). [Osborn, Name] Gen. 15:2; 1 Sam. 15:21, 30; 2 Sam. 7:18, 19, 20, 28; Ps. 68:20 could then have 'Lord Jehovah'.

But, in place of the actual name, 'the LORD' (all in capital letters) is substituted in most Bible versions in English (KJV, RV, FEN, GOS, RSV, NBV, NAB, GNB, NAS, NIV, RAV, REB, NRS, CEV), even though capital letters are obviously inaudible when read aloud (and give a misleading impression of emphasis).

A few versions use 'the Lord' (no capitals) both for the divine name and for the Hebrew word 'ǝdonay (AMP, LBP, TEB, etc). MOF uses 'the Eternal'.

So far we have talked about original proper names keeping more or less their original form in English translation. But in Mk. 1:4 above, we also observed *baptizōn*, *baptisma*, two Greek words often merely transliterated into English as 'baptizing, baptism', which is partly to avoid theological controversy (if the latter were meaningfully translated as 'immersion'). But we also find Hebrew plurals like *cherubim*, *seraphim*; *urim*, *thummim* transliterated into English because no English equivalent exists.

What we do not need, however, is the Greek *Amen, amen*, ('I say to you') reproduced in English (Jn. 3:3, 5, 11, etc. NAB 86), instead of 'I solemnly assure you' (NAB 70) or 'Truly, truly' etc. as in many versions. Likewise, we do not need *parbar* (1 Chr. 26:18 RSV); nor Hebrew measures (*bath, kor* REB) or Greek monetary units (*denarii* REB), as they do not mean anything till one refers to a table of such units at the beginning (REB). (Bratcher, REB)

7.3 CLOSE TO THE ORIGINAL SOUNDS

Occasionally, some pairs of original words sound the same as each other so that an attempt could be made not only to translate the words' meanings, but also to imitate their similar sounds. This has been done in Gen. 2:23, where the Hebrew *'ish, 'ishshah* are readily translated as 'man, woman'.

In Isa. 29:9, two Hebrew verbs of similar sounds have been translated as 'be stupefied and stunned' (NJB).

If only Isa. 5:7's similar-sounding Hebrew words with contrasting meanings could have been matched in English!

'And he looked for *mishpat* / But behold, *mispah*; //
               [justice]   [bloodshed]
For *tsedaqah*, / But behold, *tse'aqah*.'
   [righteousness]   [outcry]

In Amos 8:1–2, NIV gives 'a basket of ripe fruit' and then 'the time is ripe' to alert readers to the fact that the Hebrew original has similar-sounding words. [Ellington, Wit]

In Gen. 5:29, Moffatt has 'whom he called Noah, saying, 'Now we shall 'know a' relief from our labour . . .', where he attempted to imitate the similar-sounding Hebrew words for 'Noah' and 'relief'.

What we should not find, however, are two similar-sounding English words which do not represent two similar-sounding words of the original; for example, in Jn. 3:30, 'increase . . . decrease' (KJV) represent *auksanein . . . elattousthai*; and in Rom. 12:2, 'be conformed . . . transformed' (KJV) represent *syschematiz- . . . meta-*

morpho-, neither of which pairs of Greek words sound like each other.

7.4   CLOSE TO THE ORIGINAL GRAMMATICAL FORMS

We saw both in 3.1 and 3.2 that a better understanding of the Hebrew and Greek languages has led to better translating of the two Hebrew verbal aspects, and of the two Greek verbal aspects (which turn out to be more fundamental than the tenses which it also has). But the original languages' aspects and tenses simply do not correspond neatly with the English tenses and aspects.

Conc actually matches the Greek aorist (momentary and usually past) with the English simple present, thereby distorting the original meaning.

Neither 'With desire I have desired' (Lk. 22:15 KJV NKJ), nor 'Surely blessing I will bless you, and multiplying I will multiply you' (Heb. 6:14 NKJ), is proper English, nor was it Greek, but rather it reflects an initial Hebrew infinitive construction emphasizing the verb.

WYC1 actually had 'The Lord shall dread his adversaries' (1 Sam. 2:10) because its Latin original had object first and subject last! [Omanson, NOAB] A similar confusion was caused by Gaus in Jn. 1:1: 'and God was what the Word was'. [Bratcher, Unvarnished]

It happens, however, that older Bible versions (as well as modern ones which use older English) all preserve the basic distinction both in Hebrew and in Greek between 'you singular' and 'you plural', translated respectively as 'thou' and 'you' (see, for example, throughout Matt. chs 5–7); NWT tries to preserve this distinction in modern English by using 'you' and 'YOU' respectively, but this looks unnatural in English.

In Gal. 3:16, the whole point of the passage is the grammatical number of the nouns so that GNB has: 'The scripture does not use the plural 'descendants', meaning many people, but the singular 'descendant', meaning one person only, namely, Christ.'

The following word-for-word translations of two original

nouns joined by 'of' conceal, rather than reveal, the original meaning:

> children of the bridechamber; sons of disobedience; daughters of Jerusalem; a judge of unrighteousness (Lk. 18:6); the chastisement of our peace (Isa. 53:5); the holy of holies.

Likewise, word-for-word translations of two words joined by 'and' give the wrong impression that two things or events are referred to:

> grace and apostleship (Rom. 1:5); his understanding and answers (Lk. 2:47); of hope and resurrection of the dead (Acts 23:6); answered and said. [Beekman & Callow, chs 14, 16]

Many a long passage of the Old Testament (eg. Gen. 1) gives the impression either of being one incredibly long sentence linked together with innumerable 'and's, or of being of poor literary quality since English does not tolerate 'and' at the beginning of almost every clause. But that is the misleading impression that such word-for-word translations of 'and' create.

In the New Testament letters, Greek actually does produce incredibly-long sentences (eg. Eph. 1:3–14), simply because it has far more participles ('-ing' verbs) and infinitives ('to-' verbs) than English; but, if such a sentence is translated word-for-word, it gives abnormal English and actually obscures the original meaningful connections.

It is important to realize, before translating, that the grammatical peculiarities of one language never correspond neatly with those of any other.

7.5   CLOSE TO THE ORIGINAL WORDS

If the original repeats the same word with the same meaning in a short passage, then the translation should also repeat the same English equivalent, rather than introduce more than one equivalent (the English equivalents given in **bold** type are preferred to the equivalents in plain type):

Rom. 5:2–3
kaukhōm- × 2

NIV, RSV: **rejoice** × 2; NRS, GNB, JB: **boast** × 2; REB: **exult** × 2

NKJ: rejoice, glory; CEV: happy, gladly; TEB: happy, joy

1 Cor. 13:8, 10
katargēthēs- × 3
GOS, RSV: **pass away** × 3; NRS: **come to an end** × 3
NKJ, KJV: fail, vanish, be done away; NIV: cease, pass, disappear; GNB: temporary, pass, disappear; REB: cease, vanish, vanish

2 Cor 12:9
dynamis × 2
GOS: **strength** × 2; NIV, GNB, REB, TEB, NRS, NJB, CEV: **power** × 2
NKJ, KJV: strength, power

2 Thess. 1:6
thlib- × 3
NJB: **(inflict) hardship** × 3; NRS: **afflict(ion)** × 3;
CEV: punish, trouble(s) × 2

Isa. 51:3
niham × 2
NJB: **has pity** × 2;
TEB: comfort, show mercy

Jer. 17:14
-rapha' × 2, *-yasha'-* × 2
NJB, REB: **heal** × 2; **save** × 2;
GNB: heal, be well; rescue, be safe

Incredibly, two 'professors of Greek' (Custer & Neal) complained that GNB has 'how God puts people right with himself' (Rom. 1:17) and 'have been put right with God' (5:1), with the same word repeated; while KJV has 'righteousness of God' and 'being justified', with different words for the same Greek root (*dikaio-*). Indeed, it has been convincingly shown that only GNB (as well as the NTs: cbWi, Barc, Tran; and cf. AMP, GOS) has solved this translation problem touching an important doctrine, by consistently using the same word-family, 'right' (though early Catholic versions had tried to use only the 'just' word-family); while all other versions (WYC, TYN, KJV, NRS, NJB, REB, NIV) vary between two word-families, 'right' usually for the noun, and 'just' usually for the verb. [Moore]

Compare Gal. 3:11 in NIV and GNB respectively (my italics):

'Clearly no one is *justified* before God by the law, because, "The *righteous* will live by faith."'

'Now, it is clear that no one is *put right* with God by means of the Law, because the scripture says, "Only the person *who is put right with God* through faith shall live."'

Conversely, if a passage in the original language has two words with similar meanings, these should not be translated by just one word in English, but by two words if two are available:

Num. 10:29–30
'erets, maqom
NIV: **land, place;**
NJB: country × 2.

Isa. 49:26
moshi'a-, go'el
NJB: **saviour, redeemer;** REB: **deliverer, redeemer;**
TEB: who saves you × 2.

Gal. 6:2, 5
barē, phortion
NKJ, GNB, NIV, NRS, GOS, NJB: **burden, load;** NEB **Tran: load, burden;** JB: **trouble, burden;**
KJV, REB: burden × 2.

Since Hebrew, Greek, and English are all different languages, they vary enormously even in the numbers of words they have in their respective vocabularies; which makes nonsense of the claim in Conc (and implicitly by other word-for-word translations) that each word of the original is consistently rendered by the same English word. In any case, the words that seem to be equivalent between languages actually have completely different ranges of meaning.

For example, the Greek *phobos* could be translated literally with the English 'fear' in every context, even though its object might be ghosts (Matt. 14:26), or the

Jews (Jn. 7:13), or the Lord (Acts 9:31), or the authorities (Rom. 13:7). Must *haima* be translated just as 'blood' both in Matt. 26:28 and in Eph. 1:7? And *splangkhna* as *bowels* in Col. 3:12, Phil. 1:8, and 1 Jn. 3:17 (where KJV has to add 'of compassion' to make sense)?

And should *sarks* always be translated as 'flesh' in Lk. 24:39, 1 Cor. 6:16; 1:26; Rom. 8:1–5; 11:14; 13:14; 2 Cor. 7:5; Acts 2:17; Jn. 3:6, irrespective of the variation in original meaning from 'flesh' to 'body' to 'human standards' to 'human nature' to '(fellow)countryman' to 'sinful nature' to 'ourselves' to 'mankind' to 'physically'? [Newman, New way; Dillard S.2]

Although the Hebrew word for 'son, child' can be so translated into English in many cases, the plural form as in 'sons of Judah' or 'children of Israel' gives a completely misleading impression to English readers, because the reference is neither to 'male offspring of a parent' nor to 'juveniles', but to 'people' in each case.

Must the Hebrew *yad* always be translated as 'hand' even in Isa. 6:6 (REB) and not simply 'with' (jpsa) or 'holding' (NRS)? [Crim, NJV] The Hebrew *bet* does not just mean 'house', but its range extends to 'family, household'. And *'ab* does not just mean 'father', but also 'grandfather' and 'ancestor'. [Giese]

How meaningful are the following word-for-word translations of figures of speech? 'Gird up the loins of your mind' (1 Pet. 1:13); 'stand in the way of sinners' (Ps. 1:1 NIV); 'they put the branch to their nose' (Ezek. 8:17); 'shutteth up his bowels' (1 Jn. 3:17 KJV); 'ye have made our savour to be abhorred in the eyes of Pharaoh' (Ex. 5:21); 'how long do you lift up our soul?' (Jn. 10:24 KJ2)' . . . keep us in doubt?' (KJV).

SUMMARY

We discover that there are very few cases where the form of the original writing or sounds can be closely imitated in translation, except in the case of proper names where it is normally expected.

Since no two languages are the same in grammatical patterns or in vocabulary, we should not expect these original forms to be closely imitated in translation if the original meaning is to be faithfully transmitted.

Indeed, when a translator does not understand the full and precise meaning of a passage, he may take refuge in a word-for-word translation, thereby passing the buck of understanding the original meaning to the reader, who is much less capable of working it out. A literal translator is like an engineer whose bridge across a river goes only halfway! [Arichea; Kraft, p.22; Nida, Toward, p.192]

8

Faithful to the meaning of the original words and phrases?

Instead of crossing over nearer the surface of the two languages (shown in Figure 3 of ch. 5.3), that is, from Hebrew or Greek words to English words in word-for-word translation, a Bible translator is obliged rather to cross over near the 'deep end', preserving the full meaning of the original and re-expressing that same meaning in the other language. That re-expression should of course be 'as literal (word-for-word) as possible' if the original meaning is thereby expressed; and 'as free (meaning-for-meaning) as necessary' to express that original meaning.

8.1   DIFFERENT RANGES OF WORD-MEANING

Most concepts do not have clearcut boundaries. A concept is best thought of as a range of meaning with a 'prototypical' (clear case) centre and variable extensions from that centre; eg. in most cultures, 'father' is prototypically the 'male parent', but may or may not be extendable in a particular culture to include 'grandfather, ancestor, uncle, originator, priest', etc. But the chances that two corresponding concepts from two cultures will exactly coincide are remote—partial overlapping is all we can ever expect.

Therefore, a single Hebrew or Greek word occurring in many different contexts is very unlikely to be translatable by the same English word in all these contexts. Even Young, who criticizes KJV for translating the one Hebrew verb *nathan* by sixty-seven English words, has to use ten English words in his very Literal Translation!

So the Greek *sarks* may be translated (mostly NIV) as 'flesh and bones' (Lk. 24:39); as 'a human being' (Jn. 1:14 GNB); 'my own people' (Rom. 11:14; cf Acts 2:17); 'human nature' (Rom. 1:3), 'by human standards' (1 Cor. 1:26); 'from a worldly point of view' (2 Cor. 5:16), 'the world' (2 Cor. 10:3); 'sinful nature' (Rom. 8:3; 13:14); 'body' (2 Cor. 7:5; Col. 1:22). [Fee & Stuart, p.39, 41]

Phobos may be translated according to context as 'fear, reverence, respect'; *pneuma* as 'wind, spirit' in Jn. 3:6–8; 'doulos' as 'slave, servant, boy'.

The Hebrew *nephesh* may be translated according to context as 'breath, soul, life, mind, living thing, animal, person, self'. [Nida, God's Word, p.65–6]

However, in one context, a word has only one meaning, so that AMP is wrong to list in one context all the meanings the word may also have in other contexts.

8.2 THE RIGHT WORD-MEANING

Every culture has its own concepts denoted by the words of the appropriate language, rather like geographical features symbolized on a map. When two cultures are relatively similar to each other, their respective concepts substantially overlap and so are more readily translatable, even word for word. But the less similar two cultures are, like the ancient biblical cultures and modern European cultures, the less overlap we are likely to find, and so less easy translatability.

Even when it is relatively easy, care should still be taken to get the right equivalent word: (In each case below, * is used to indicate an original literal meaning; and the English equivalents given in **bold** type are preferred to the equivalents in plain type.)

Matt. 2:23; Jn. 6:1,16
thalassa
NJB: sea;
CEV: **lake.** (because of size, location)

Ps. 23:4
hesed (*covenant love)

KJV: mercy;
NIV: **love.**

Matt. 5:16
anthrōpōn (both sexes)
NIV: men;
GNB: **people.**

2 Tim. 1:7
deilia
NAB, REB, NRS: **cowardly/ice;** NIV, JNB: **timidity;**
KJV: fear.

Various OT *contexts*
RSV: Great/Western Sea;
TEB: **Mediterranean Sea.** (modern name)

Ps. 9:17; Job 11:8
she'ol (*abode of the dead)
KJV: hell;
NIV, NRS: **grave.**

Acts 28:1
Melitē
KJV: Melita;
RSV: **Malta.** (the modern name)

Matt. 2:1
magoi
NAS, NIV: magi, Magi; NRS: wise men;
REB: **astrologers;** GNB: **men who studied the stars.**

Jos. 8 & 13–21 etc.
'ir
KJV, GNB: city;
NIV: **town.** (because of population)

Prov. 19:21; 1 Ki. 10:24
leb (*organ of thought)
KJ2, NJB, NIV: heart;
NRS, REB: **mind.**

1 Cor. 13.
agapē (*Christian love)
KJV: charity;
GEN etc: **love.**

Deut. 10:3
luhoth
KJV, AMP: stone tables;

NIV, GNB: **stone tablets.**
John 14:2
monai
KJV: mansions;
GEN, NRS: **dwelling places;** TEB: **rooms**.

In Matt. 11:28, does 'you who *labour*' (RSV) not suggest either childbirth or heavy manual work, rather than tiredness (GNB) or weariness (NIV), which are closer to the original meaning, and also relevant to modern readers?

Schonfield 1985 replaced 'familiar ecclesiastical terms': [Bratcher, Original]
baptism   church   apostle bishop   deacon
immersion community envoy supervisor administrator

As we saw in ch. 3, increasing knowledge of the original languages has led to more accurate translation of their verbal tenses and aspects, especially NAS, NWT, NIV, Barc, cbWi.

Matt. 3:14 (imperfect) progressive aspect
NIV: **tried to deter;**
KJV: forbad.

Matt. 25:8 (present) progressive aspect
NJB, REB: **are going out;**
KJV: are gone out.

Rom. 6:4
(aorist) past momentary
NIV: **were buried;**
KJV: are buried.

Acts 4:34 (imperfect) progressive aspect
GNB: **would sell;**
RSV: sold.

1 Cor. 1:18 (present) progressive aspect
GNB (NIV): **being lost . . . being saved;**
KJV, JND: that perish . . . which are saved.

Matt. 14:30 (aorist) past momentary
NAS: **became afraid;**
NIV, GNB: was afraid.

Luke 5:6 (imperfect) progressive aspect
RV, NKJ, RSV, NIV: **were breaking; began to break;**

KJV: brake.

Jn. 5:18 (imperfect) progressive aspect
NIV: **tried . . . was he breaking** the Sabbath, but he **was even calling** God his own Father;
KJV: *sought . . . had broken* the sabbath, but *said* also that God was his Father.

Lk. 9:49 (imperfect) progressive aspect
NJB, REB: **we tried to stop him;**
BLE: we stopped him; KJ2: we forbade him; AMP: we commanded him to stop.

When it comes to measures of weight, capacity, and length, the original 'ephah', 'homer', 'bath', 'shekel', 'talent' etc. (KJV RSV NRS) are far from meaningful in an English translation (unless the reader takes the trouble to look up some Table of Weights and Measures). Neither are the archaic 'cubit', 'span' (KJV, RSV, NAS, NIV). The only meaningful possibilities are either the obsolescent 'pound' (weight), 'quart', 'foot' (NBV, TEB), or the innovating 'kilogramme', 'litre', 'metre' (despite the apparent anachronism), together with the original units in footnotes if necessary. [Fry; Nida, Good News, ch. 8]

In Lk. 24:13, the original '60 stadia' could well come out as 'about seven miles' (RSV, GNB), preserving the round figure after the accurate calculation.

The case is slightly different with units of money, The original 'shekel', 'talent', 'mina', 'denarius' could be turned into 'pounds', 'dollars', 'pence', 'cents'; but the full original meaning depends very often on the actual value, so that in Mk. 14:5 we could have 'a year's wages' (NIV, NAB86) instead of '300 denarii' (NJB); in Matt. 18:24, 28 we could have 'dollars, dollars' (GNB), instead of 'talents', 'denarii' (NAS); in Rev. 6:6: 'four cups of wheat will sell for twenty cents' (Cres), instead of 'a choinix of wheat for a denarius' (AMP) [Fee & Stuart, p 38; Nida, Quality]

Since the meanings of proper names, both of places and of people (eg. Eve, Jacob, Beer-Sheba), are often important especially in the Old Testament, and are automatically known to the original Hebrew-speaking readers, such meanings should be given in the translation, either in the text itself, possibly with a footnote of the original form of the name (Jos. 7:24, 26 'Devastation Valley' Anchor, 'Valley of Trouble' TEB; 1 Sam. 23:28 'Dividing Rock' REB, 'Rock of Escape' NRS, 'Gorge of Separations' NJB); or in parentheses or italics immediately after the original name (Gen. 30:6–24 BLE); but hardly with the original name in the text, plus a footnote of the meaning (Jos. 7:24, 26 'Valley of Achor' NRS, REB, NIV, NJB; 1 Sam. 23:28 'Sela Hammahlekoth' NIV). [Omanson, Name; Ellington, Wit]

8.3   THE RIGHT PHRASE-MEANING

Word-for-word translations of Hebrew and Greek figures of speech, and indeed many other not uncommon phrases, often come out in English either with no meaning or the wrong meaning. [Nida & Taber, p.87–9, 106–7; Wonderly, ch. 12; Beekman & Callow, ch. 7; Nida, Good News, ch. 6]

Lk 15:20
KJV, RAV: *fell on his neck
RSV: **embraced him;** NRS: **put his arms around him**

Ps. 23:5
NIV: *anoint my head with oil;
GNB: **welcome me as an honored guest**

Ezek. 8:17
NRS NIV: *they put the branch to their nose;
GNB: **they insult me in the most offensive way possible**

1 Cor. 7:1
NRS, NAB86: *touch a woman; NIV, LBP, GNB: marry;
NAB70: **have relations with a woman** [Fee & Stuart, p.38]

Gen. 31:35
NAS (KJV, RSV) the manner of women is upon me;
NIV (GNB): **I'm having my period**

Jn. 14:1
NRS: *do not let your hearts be troubled;
GNB: **do not be worried and upset**

Jn. 9:24
NRS: *Give glory to God!; RSV: *Give God the praise!

GNB: **Promise before God that you will tell the truth!**

Ex. 32:29
NWT: *fill your hands; BLE: do your devoir(!)
KJV LTB: **consecrated yourselves . . .;** NRS: **ordained yourselves for service**

Lk. 20:34
NJB: *The children of this world take wives and;
NIV: **The people of this age marry and . . .;**
TEB: **On earth, people marry each other;**
NRS: **Those who belong to this age marry.**

1 Ki. 6:34
NJB: and the two leaves of juniper;
REB: **and a double door of pine, each leaf . . .**

Ex. 16:6
KJV: *the children of Israel;
RSV: **the people of Israel;**
NRS, GNB: **the Israelites.**

1 Ki. 7:23
KJV, NRS: molten sea(!);
GNB: **round tank of bronze;** TEB: **a large round bowl from bronze.**

Amos 1:2
NRS: *for three transgressions and for four;
GNB: **have sinned again and again**

Ps. 23:6
YOU: *for a length of days; NIV, KJV: forever; NJB: for all time to come
GNB: **as long as I live;** REB: **throughout the years to come**

Ps. 1:1
NIV (KJ2): *stand in the way of sinners; NAB: walks in the way of . . .;
TEB: **go where sinners go;** NRS, REB: **take/follow the path that sinners tread;** GNB: **follow the example of sinners.**

Mk. 2:19
KJV: *children of the bridechamber;
REB: **the bridegroom's friends;** NRS: **the wedding guests**

Eph. 2:2
NAS: *sons of disobedience; KJV: children of disobedience;
NRS, NIV: **those who are disobedient;** GNB: **the people who disobey God;** REB: **God's rebel subjects**

Eph. 3:21
YOU: *of the age of the ages; BLE: . . . of endless time; KJ2: . . . of the age forever;
NRS, NIV, NAB, NWT, GNB: **for ever and ever**

1 Pet. 1:13
KJV, RAV: *gird up the loins of your mind;
NRS: **prepare your minds for action;** NWT: **brace up** YOUR **minds for activity;** TEB: **prepare your minds for service;** GNB: **have your minds ready for action.**

Lk. 18:6
KJV: *a judge of unrighteousness;
REB, NRS: **the unjust judge**

1 Tim. 5:10
NAS, NRS: (she has) washed the saints' feet; NIV: washing the feet of the saints; REB: by washing the feet of God's people;
GNB: **performed humbled duties for other Christians;** CEV: **welcoming God's people into her home**

8.4 EXPANDING TO CONVEY THE ORIGINAL MEANING

A concept familiar to one culture is normally denoted by a single word in that language. But, when translated into the language of a different culture, a single word may not be available, and so some longer expression might have to be used to convey the original meaning. [Beekman & Callow, ch. 13]

In modern English versions, the word 'you' is used both for singular and for plural, whereas the original languages used two different forms, as was also the case in earlier English (KJV, etc). The distinction could be preserved by always capitalizing the plural form (NWT); or occasionally by adding a distinguishing word; eg. in 1 Cor. 3:16 'you yourselves', Lk. 22:32 'you, Simon', both NIV. [Andersons, p.5]

Eph. 1:2 etc
hagioi (*holy men)
KJV, NRS, NIV: the saints; NAB: the holy ones; NJB TEB: God's holy people;
GNB, REB: **God's people.**

Gen. 4:1, 17, 25; 16:4; *etc*
NRS: *knew;
NIV: **lay with;** GNB: **had intercourse with.**

1 Sam. 15:29
hinnahem
KJV KJ2: repent;
NAS, NRS: **change his mind**

1 Pet. 1:18
patroparadotou
YOU: delivered by fathers;
KJV: **received by tradition from your fathers;** NIV: **handed down to you from your forefathers**

Lev. 18:16–18
NRS: *uncover the nakedness of;
NIV: **have sexual relations with.**

Jos. 6:17
herem le YHWH
KJV: accursed to the LORD; YOU: devoted to Jehovah;
NRS: **devoted to the Lord for destruction**

Matt. 5:41
angareu-
KJV: compel . . . to go; NRS: force . . . to go with him;
GNB: **one of the occupation troops forces . . . to carry his pack.**

Ruth 4:13
RSV: *he went in to her; jpsa: he cohabited with her;
NRS, NJB, REB: **they came together**

Jer. 10:16
NJB: portion of Jacob;
REB: **chosen God of Jacob;** GNB: **God of Jacob**

Metaphors, such as 'You cows of Bashan' (Amos 4:1 NRS), could be expanded into similes, such as 'You women . . . who grow fat like the well-fed cows of Bashan' (GNB), with the point of comparison made explicit.

But the most striking difference between word-for-word and meaning-for-meaning translations is in the area of technical terms, like 'faith', 'grace', 'redemption', 'atonement', 'reconciliation', 'salvation', 'sanctification', which theologians habitually use as shorthand for theological concepts. Well-instructed Christians may (or may not) understand the full implications of these terms, however familiar the terms are to them; but new Christians or non-Christians certainly cannot.

In any case, if the original 'redeem' is translated as 'pay the price for undeserving sinful people, by means of Christ's death on the cross, so as to free them from the bondage of sin and death' (Sjölander, Religious), can anyone complain that the full original meaning is not clearly translated?!

Not surprisingly, simplified Bible translations (TEB, ETR, Simp, Ledy, Cres) use this procedure for many such terms:

*Fast: Ledy: go without food so as to pray better.
*Synagogue: worship-house of the Jews.
*Parable: Ledy: picture-story.
High places: TEB: places where false gods were worshipped.

8.5   OTHER HELPS TO CONVEY MEANING

Meaning which was implicit in the original may be made explicit within the text of some Bible translations, usually without any indication of what exactly has been made explicit, mainly because it is virtually impossible to be consistent and exhaustive in so indicating.

To enable readers of the translation to understand at once what the original readers already understood implicitly, we may have, instead of just 'Jordan', 'River Jordan' (not nation); or instead of 'Asia' (2 Cor. 1:8 NRS), '*province of* Asia' (GNB) (not continent); or instead of 'Chemosh' (Jer. 48:7), '*your god* Chemosh' (GNB); or instead of 'city of David', 'the city *where David was born/ruled in the past*' (not where he lives now).

However, where there is a need to make such an indication, the best method is to use half-brackets, as occasionally in NIV, ETR; or square brackets [. . .], as sometimes in JND, NWT, NBV, LBP, Stern, NAB 86?; or (*parenthesized italics*) for clarification, as in ETR: 'He tore his robe (*in anger*)'.

The tradition of using italics for such supplied material (as in GEN, KJV, RV, YOU, NAS, RAV=NKJ, KJ2, Simple) is most unfortunate as most people connect italics with emphasis (which is the diametric opposite of this other usage!).

The most striking method of making what was implicit to the original reader explicit to the reader of the translation is the use of illustrations, whether drawings or photographs, maps or plans, so that the reader can appreciate some unfamiliar object, place, or custom; eg. a flat-roofed house; the temple or tabernacle; Jerusalem city; eating at table; winnowing grain. [RSV, ed. Stirling; Nida, Good News, ch. 2–3; Quality]

What are much commoner are annotations, placed below or in the margin of the translated text. These may be used, not only to explain alternative texts (see ch. 4), but also to give alternative translations of the original, or even to admit that the original is unclear. It is much more honest to admit these facts of translatability, than to imply that everything is perfectly clear by giving no such notes.

Annotation is also used to explain what is meant, so that the reader gets to a similar state of knowledge as the reader of the original: [Osborn, Footnotes]

> **plays on words**: 'wind, spirit' (Jn. 3); 'covenant, testament' (Heb. 9:15–7);
>
> meanings of **proper names**: 'Jesus' (Matt. 1:21); 'Peter' (Matt. 16:18); 'Adam, Eve' (Gen. 3:20); 'Gibeah' (Hos. 9:9; 10:9) GNB note; Micah 1:10–5 (NIV);
>
> explanations of **unfamiliar objects**: 'mandrakes' (Gen. 30:14–6); 'ephod' (Ex. 25:7); alabaster; stocks; roof of house (Prov. 23:24; Acts 10:9);
>
> of **institutions**: Sanhedrin; synagogue; Emperor; Gentiles;
>
> of **social groups**: Herodians; tax-collectors; 'Pharisees: . . . were a Jewish religious group that followed the Old Testament and other Jewish laws and customs very carefully.' (ETR);
>
> of **customs**: circumcision; covenant; passover; burial;

marriage; vows; eating at table; 'propitiation' (Rom. 3:25 KJV) or 'sacrifice of atonement' (NIV), with footnote 'one who had turned aside wrath, taking away sin'.

Since most modern Bible readers have no access to any information on biblical culture other than the Bible itself, they would also welcome further information of historical events, of important personalities; and of dates.

8.6 MORE THAN, OR LESS THAN, THE ORIGINAL MEANING

Throughout this chapter, we have tried to show that various versions have tried to translate the full original meaning of the Bible texts with varying degrees of faithfulness. But, in striving for meaningfulness, some translations may have gone too far, or not far enough, in respect of the original meaning.

Meaning which is not original seems to have been added in some cases. In Matt. 2:13, 20, 21, AMP inexplicably repeats '(tenderly)' before 'take, took'; and in Matt. 5:3 (and throughout the Beatitudes!), to 'Blessed' AMP adds '—happy, to be envied and spiritually prosperous (that is, with life-joy and satisfaction in God's favor and salvation, regardless of their outward conditions) . . .'. in 1 Tim. 3:1, LBP has 'church leader, presiding elder' in a footnote, but 'pastor' in the text.

One example from LBP illustrates both addition to, and subtraction from, the original meaning:

> Jn. 1:17: For Moses gave us only the Law [with its rigid demands and merciless justice], while Jesus Christ brought us loving forgiveness as well.

To the original meaning LBP has added the seven words in [. . .], while the original 'grace and truth' has been reduced to only 'loving forgiveness', with nothing representing 'truth' at all!

Original meaning can also be subtracted in some cases. in 1 Cor. 15:41, CEV omits the equivalent of 'glory' four times, though the same word comes out as 'beauty' in v.43; in 2 Thess. 2:2, CEV puts 'day of' in a footnote, but only 'the Lord' in the text; in 1 Tim. 6:2, CEV has 'followers', but why not 'believers' (NJB) or even 'Christians' (LBP)? The original 'brethren' could be modernized to 'brothers' (TEB, NIV), and then to 'brothers and sisters' which is cumbersome; but something is lost when we have merely 'friends' (CEV,REB, NRS).

9

Faithful to the meaning of the original sentences?

Languages express meaning not only in words and phrases (as we saw in ch. 8), but also in clauses (which are the same as simple sentences) and in more complex sentences, to which we now turn. In each case below, the English equivalents given in **bold** type are preferred to the equivalents in plain type.

Some clauses can be misunderstood if the subjects and objects or complements are not clearly translated; for example,

Matt. 26:27
KJV: Drink ye all of it; KJ2: Drink all of it (!);
NIV: **Drink from it, all of you;** NKJ: **All of you drink from it.**

Jn. 4:2
KJV, NKJ: Though Jesus himself baptized not, but his disciples;
GNB: **Actually, Jesus himself did not baptize anyone; only his disciples did.**

Heb. 1:7
NAB 86: Of the angels he says: 'He makes his angels winds / and his ministers a fiery flame';
NJB: **To the angels, he says:** *appointing the winds his messengers and flames of fire his servants,*

Now compare a very word-for-word version (KJ2) of Gal. 5:19–21 with a more meaningful version, Simp, (set out in very short lines, as shown by /):

KJ2:	Simple:
Now the works of the flesh are clearly revealed:	Human nature does things which are wrong. These are clear:
adultery, fornication, uncleanness,	committing sexual sin / not being pure /
lustfulness, idolatry,	having orgies / worshipping false gods /
sorcery, hatreds, fightings,	practicing witchcraft / hating people / making trouble /
jealousies, angers,	being jealous / becoming too angry /
rivalries, divisions,	being selfish / making people angry with each other /
heresies, envyings, [murders,]	causing divisions / envying others /
drunkennesses, wild parties,	getting drunk / having wild parties /
and things like these; . . .	and other such things.

It is true that Greek nouns have been largely translated by verbs in the right-hand version; but is the original meaning not thereby made clearer, with some verb objects made explicit?

In reference to NIV, J P Green says: 'There is a cavalier attitude in regard to the grammatical construction of the Bible. Nouns, verbs, pronouns, adjectives and adverbs are scrambled without any respect to the original God-breathed *words*. . . . Sentences are broken up, and *words* added, in such a way as to change the meaning of the original Greek *words*.' (p.2, CLW 4.2, 1992; my italics)

This demonstrates Green's fanatical attachment to words, as if God did not inspire the original meaning, expressed in the original sentences, and indeed in the whole Scripture. We must insist that it is God's original meaning that must be translated, and not merely the words.

9.1   FAITHFUL TRANSLATION OF EVENTS AND STATES

It is of fundamental importance to any translator to realize that not every noun of Greek (or English, or any language) represents a 'person, or place, or thing', as we may have learned at school. But some nouns, like those exemplified just above, often called 'abstract', represent events (actions, processes) or states (qualities) with their actual participants left implicit. Such nouns can then be translated into corresponding verbs, together with explicit subjects and objects as participants. For one thing, in any language, the full original meaning can thus be more clearly expressed; and, in some languages including common English, it is more natural to express actions and states by verbs.

In all the examples following, the original event or state is italicized.

> *2 Cor. 5:18*
> NRS: . . . God, who *reconciled* us to himself through Christ, and has given us the ministry of *reconciliation*;
> GNB: God, who through Christ *changed us from enemies into his friends* and gave us the task of *making others his friends* also.

In Matt. 26:28, 'This is my blood' is an appropriate translation because Jesus has just presented the graphic symbolism of the red wine. But in Eph. 1:7; 2:13 the noun '*blood*' could more meaningfully be translated as 'the *shedding of his blood*' (REB), 'the *blood of his death*' (TEB), 'his *death*' (GNB 76), referring to the great event of Christ's *death* on the cross. Likewise, in Rom. 5:9 we could have 'by Christ's *sacrificial death*' (REB).

All this applies to traditional theological terms like '*salvation*' which is basically 'God *saves* people'; or '*grace*' which is basically 'God is *kind to* us in a way we do not deserve' (CEV).

Far from 'divesting the (theological) term of its significance', this procedure rather increases its significance, both for those who have not met it before and for those who are familiar with the tradition.

Heb. 1:3 (see Tables in ch.6)
RAV, NIV: brightness, *radiance*;
GNB, **Tran:** *reflects, radiates*; LBP, ETR: *shines out with, shows.*

2 Tim. 4:6
NAS: the time of my *departure* has come;
GNB: **the time is here for me** *to leave this life.*

Rom. 9:8
NRS: children *of the flesh* . . . children *of the* promise;
GNB: **children** *born in the usual way* . . . *born as a result of God's promise.*

Heb. 1:3
RAV: the word of his *power*;
NRS: **his** *powerful* **word**; NJB: **his** *powerful* **command.**

Gal. 2:2
RAV: by *revelation*;
NRS: in response to a *revelation*;
GNB: **because God** *revealed* **to me that I should go.**

Heb. 1:3
RAV, ETR: *express image, perfect copy*; NIV: *exact representation*;
MOF: *stamped with* God's own character; Tran: *shows us exactly what* God's nature is; LBP: all that (he) is and does *marks* him as God

Rom. 1:17
NRS: the *righteousness* of God; GNB: **how God** *puts people right* **with himself.**

1 Tim. 3:6
NRS: fall into the *condemnation* of the devil;
GNB: **be** *condemned*, **as the Devil was.**

Heb. 9:7
RSV: the errors of the people; NJB: the people's *faults of inadvertence*;
NRS: *sins committed unintentionally . . .*; GNB: **sins which [they] have committed without knowing they were sinning**

9.2 TRANSLATING MULTIPLE EVENTS AND STATES

Let us first clear out of the way a common mistake made by word-for-word translations: that is, indicating two events where there is in fact only one; for example, 'answered and said' should be translated as a single event: 'said in answer' or 'answered'. Lk. 2:47: 'his understanding and his answers'(NRS) could be 'his intelligent answers' (GNB).

Something similar can be seen when two abstract nouns are joined by 'and', when they may be translated as if they are two separate things, rather than the second event as the content of the first event; for example, Rom. 1:5: 'grace and apostleship' (NRS) should be 'the privilege of being an apostle' (GNB); Acts 23:6: 'hope and resurrection of the dead' (RAV) should be 'hope of the resurrection of the dead' (NRS).

In Heb. 1:3, the Greek has an abstract noun-phrase 'cleansing of-the sins' followed by a verbal participle 'having-acquired', which totals two events, which should therefore not be translated: 'purged'; (KJV, RAV), 'made clean' (ETR), 'cleansed' (NAB 70); but rather, 'After he had provided / purification from sins' (NIV), or 'When he had made it possible for man to be cleansed from sin' (Tran), with 'he' and 'man' made explicit.

But we sometimes also find two events or states, represented by one abstract noun in the original: 'repentance' means 'someone sinned and then turned from sin' (CEV); while 'forgiveness' means 'A sinned against B, and then B lets A off''.

Mk. 1:4
NRS: *proclaiming a baptism of repentance for the forgiveness of sins;*
GNB: **'Turn away from your sins and be baptized,' he told the people, 'and God will forgive your sins.';** ETR: **He told the people to be baptized to show they wanted to change their lives. Then their sins would be forgiven.**

In the middle version, 'people' and 'God' are made

explicit as subjects and objects of verbs, while in the upper version both are left implicit.

Matt. 3:8
NRS: bear *fruit* worthy of *repentance*
TEB: **You must *do the things which show* that you really have *changed your hearts and lives*;** GNB: ***Do those things that will show* that you have *turned from your sins***

Lk. 8:48
NIV: Your *faith* has *healed* you;
ETR: **You are *made well* because you *believed***

Isa. 53:5
RAV: The *chastisement* of our *peace* was upon him;
GNB: **We *are healed* by the *punishment he suffered*;** NRS: **upon him was the *punishment* that *made us whole***

Rom. 1:5
RAV: for *obedience* to the *faith* among all nations;
GNB: **in order to lead people of all nations to *believe* and *obey***

9.3   YOU CANNOT SEE THE TREES FOR THE FOREST!

The 'forest' of the title refers to the extremely long sentences which are often found in the original Greek, especially of Paul's letters; eg. Eph. 1:3–14; 1 Cor. 5:5–10; Heb. 1:1–4; Acts 1:1–5. The sentences are long because Greek has far more participles and infinitives ('-ing' and 'to-' verbs) than most languages, as well as many abstract nouns and relative ('who, which') clauses.

So, a word-for-word translation of such sentences is almost incomprehensible in English, with the result that the reader gets lost in the interminable sentence ('forest'), unable to appreciate the meaningful connections among the component clauses ('trees').

Eph. 1:3–14 becomes two sentences in KJV; but the meaningful connections are clearer in the seven or eight sentences and two paragraphs of NIV and REB, and in the fifteen sentences and five paragraphs of GNB.

Heb. 1:1–4 (refer to vs 1–3 quoted in the Tables of ch. 6)

consists of one Greek sentence of seventy-two words, the connections being reproduced below as in the word-for-word DOU version (main verbs capitalized): ' . . . speaking . . . HATH SPOKEN . . . whom . . . by whom . . . also . . . who . . . being . . . and carrying . . . making . . . SITTETH . . . being made . . . as . . . then . . .'

In 1.1, very few versions imitate the Greek participle (JND, YOU, FEN, West, Spen, Conc); some introduce yet another who-clause (KJV, RAV, NWT); some introduce a when/after clause (NAS, REB); but most start with a main clause with 'spoke' (CEV, NRS, TEB, KJ2, NAB, NJB, NIV, GNB).

However, the contrast between the first two clauses should be marked either with 'whereas' at the very beginning (ROT), or by 'but' between the clauses (CEV, REB, NRS, NJB, NIV, GNB, LBP).

In 1:3a, the initial connection is clearer with simply a new sentence (CEV, REB, NRS, TEB, NIV, GNB) or with 'for' (LAM), than with 'who being' (RAV, KJ2, BLE).

In 1:3b, the participle 'making' (Conc, CHA, DOU) is wrong, while 'having made' etc (KJ2, Cass, jbP2, Wues) is unclear; 'when, after, now that' (CEV, REB, NRS, NAS, NAB, NJB, RAV, NIV, GNB) is much clearer. No visible link (TEB, Cres, Ledy, Beck, Noli) also leaves the connection obscure.

In Lk. 1:1, KJV starts with 'forasmuch', while GNB has 'and so' (1:3), to mark the same connection between clauses.

In Matt. 11:29, GEN has 'Take my yoke on you, and learne of me that I am meeke and lowly in heart:', indicating the object-clause of the verb (also CCB); a few versions have no conjunction (KNO Cres Beck Ledy); but the vast majority have 'for'—to me, inexplicably!

It is only in some of the more modern versions, which are neither too word-for-word nor too simplified, that the connections between clauses are translated seriously, so that readers can appreciate the original meaningful connections between clauses and sentences within paragraphs. [Wonderly, ch. 15; Nida, Good News, ch. 7; Beekman & Callow, ch. 18 & Ap.D]

9.4   YOU CANNOT SEE THE FOREST FOR THE TREES!

The 'trees' of the title refer to the innumerable clauses (each starting with the Hebrew *w* 'and') which form the very stuff of Hebrew prose. Word-for-word translations translate every *w* with 'and', even though it is virtually the equivalent of the use of capitalization at the beginning of English sentences [Fee & Stuart, p.40–1]; or a comma or semicolon at the end of the preceding clause.

Even the book of Leviticus begins with 'and' in KJV; in Gen. 1, every verse (plus many other parts of verses) begins with the same 'and' in KJV (except v.27 'so'); RSV has two 'so', one 'then' and four zero; NIV keeps twelve 'and', while NRS has ten; PUR however had only two 'and', while REB has three; and GNB has only 'one'. The chaining together of innumerable clauses with 'and'— actually, a grand total of sixty-two in Gen. 1—makes understanding of the text as a whole very difficult, especially for English readers, who associate such writing with small children.

A translation of Gen. 1:1–3 avoiding 'and' and preserving the meaningful connections between clauses might be: 'When God began to create the universe, the earth was still formless and desolate while the ocean was shrouded in darkness, though a wind from God had started moving over the waters. Then God commanded, "Let light come into being!" '(cf. NRS, NEB, GNB, NAB, LBP, GOS).

In 1 Chr. 17:1; 18:1; 19:1; Lk. 2:1, KJV, RV, JND, etc. all have 'And it came to pass (that) . . .', which is the best-known example of 'biblical' English, even yielding misguided sermons on the temporary nature of things! Most modern versions correctly agree to omit any word-for-word equivalent, as it merely serves, like 'After this', to introduce a new episode.

Prov. 16:3
NRS: Commit your work to the Lord, / *and* your plans will be established;

If you commit your work to the Lord, your plans will be established. [Nida, Fewer, p.134–7]

Prov. 27:22
NRS: Crush a fool in a mortar with a pestle . . ., but the folly
will not be driven out of him;
   Even if you crush a fool . . ., he will *nevertheless* continue
to act like a fool;
   RAV: *Though* you grind a fool . . ., *yet* his foolishness will
not depart from him.

The above examples indicate that a translator who
understands the meaningful connections between Hebrew
clauses should use the normal range of English conjunctions.

The same observation can apply to some New Testament
Greek (which imitates the Hebrew): in Jn. 6:49, NRS has
'Your ancestors ate the manna in the wilderness, and
they died.', as if the manna was poisonous! The conjunction should rather be 'but' or 'yet' (GNB, NIV).

9.5 MORE THAN, OR LESS THAN, THE ORIGINAL MEANING

Throughout this chapter, we have shown that various
versions have tried to translate the full original meaning
of the Bible texts with varying degrees of faithfulness.
But, in striving for meaningfulness, some translations
may have gone too far, or not far enough, in respect of
the original meaning.

Meaning which is not original seems to have been
added in some cases: (* indicates the original meaning).

Rom. 3:21–2
*faith
LBP: if we trust [Jesus Christ to take away our sins]

The original meaning seems to have been changed in
other cases:

Matt. 5:5
*inherit the earth
CEV: **The earth will belong to them!**;
GNB: receive what God has promised.

Rom. 1:16–17
*the righteousness of God
LBP: making us ready for heaven.

Rom. 2:4
GNB: ***repent;**
CEV: turn to (God).

Rom. 14:23
*not from faith
CEV: against your beliefs.

Jn. 3:6
NAB2: **What is born of flesh is flesh and what is born of spirit is spirit;**
CEV: **Humans give life to their children. Yet only God's Spirit can change you into a child of God.**

Jn. 4:2-4
NAB2: and those who worship him must worship **in Spirit and truth;**
GNB: and only by the power of his Spirit can people worship him as he really is; CEV: and those who worship God must be led by the Spirit to worship him according to the truth.

Jn. 3:8
NAB2: **so it is with everyone who is born of the Spirit;**
CEV: Only God's Spirit gives new life.

Matt. 7:12
NIV (jbP2): ***this sums up the Law and the Prophets;**
jbP1: this is the essence of all true religion [Carson, Limits].

Rom. 6:13
NRS: *present your members **to God as instruments of righteousness;** TEB: Offer the parts of your body **to God to be used for doing good;** GNB: surrender your whole being **to him to be used for righteous purposes;**
CEV: Make every part of your body a slave that pleases God.

In 1 Tim. 3:15, CEV does not equate 'God's family' (or 'house') with 'the church' (as in Greek).

Original meaning can also be subtracted in some cases:

Rom. 6:19
NRS: ***to impurity and to greater and greater iniquity;**
CEV: of your evil thoughts.

1 Cor. 13:11
*talked like a child
CEV: —

Jn. 3:4b
NAB2: **Surely he cannot reenter his mother's womb and be born again, can he?;**
CEV: —

2 Cor. 8:9

GNB:	CEV:
You know	You know
the grace	that our Lord Jesus Christ
of our Lord Jesus Christ;	was kind enough
rich as he was,	to give up all his riches
he made himself poor	and become poor,
for your sake	
in order to make you rich	so that you could become rich.
by means of his poverty.	

Jn. 4:15c
NAB2: so that **I may not be thirsty or** have to keep coming here to draw water;
CEV: Then I won't have to come to this well again.

Some versions seem to go too far from the original meaning, whether explicit or implicit, and add something of their own meaning (AMP, LBP, Barc, jbP1, especially Peterson), however attractive that might seem to their intended audience. Such extra meaning can appear also in certain types of devotional or denominational footnotes (NBV; TYN, GEN, DOU, CCB).

CONCLUSIONS FROM CHAPTERS 5–9

In chapters 3 and 4, we discussed Bible translators' increasing knowledge of the biblical cultures and languages and their increasingly enlightened use of the original manuscript evidence. But we concluded that these achievements do not make substantial differences to the overall quality of Bible translations.

In marked contrast, from chapters 5 through 9, we have seen very substantial differences in Bible translations, as you can see by glancing down the innumerable versions of Hebrews 1:1·3 displayed in chapter

6 and observing their similarities and differences.

It all depends on whether the translators try to reproduce closely the original form in relatively word-for-word translations—the most extreme examples being WY1, DOU, YOU, ROT; Conc; or they try to communicate faithfully the full original meaning in relatively meaning-for-meaning translations—the best examples being REB, NJB, GNB; Tran.

Fully meaningful translations involve not only picking the right English word for a Hebrew or Greek word, but also varying that English word according to the varying contexts; and, if there is no clear English equivalent word, expanding it to a suitable phrase to express the original meaning. All this assumes that the translator understands the full original meaning and can make the implicit participants in events and states explicit in particular contexts, especially in the case of original abstract nouns. At the same time, the translator has to understand and translate appropriately the meaningful connections between clauses and sentences, so that readers do not lose the thread of the discourse.

Is the English Adequate?

10

How natural is the English?

If you look again at Figures 3 and 4 in chapter 5, you will see that by chapter 9 we have progressed through the spelling and the wording of the originals to the underlying meaning. If we were to stop there, it would be like leading a blind man halfway across a busy street and leaving him there! [K Callow, p.9–10]

But we do not stop in that original meaning. Rather, we continue across to re-express that same meaning in the wording and spelling of the English language. Since the written and grammatical forms of the Hebrew, the Greek, and the English languages are not at all close to each other, this involves considerable re-structuring or re-wording, even in a word-for-word translation.

10.1 NATURAL ENGLISH

As far as we know, the Bible was originally written in natural Hebrew, Aramaic, and Greek. But, if the translator imitates the words and constructions of the original languages with an artificial 'translationese' English, he is actually misrepresenting the naturalness of the original languages. What is more, people may be put off from reading such an unnatural, unidiomatic Bible version more by the strangeness of the English than by the strangeness of the gospel!

Martin Luther wrote: 'Whoever would speak German must not use Hebrew style. Rather he must see to it once he understands the Hebrew author that he concentrates on the sense of the text, asking himself, "Pray tell, what do the Germans say in such a situation?" Once he has the German words to serve the purpose, let him drop the Hebrew words and express the meaning freely in the best German he knows.' [Newman, Biblical poetry]

This means that, if the English is to sound as normal, idiomatic, or natural to the readers of the translation as the original languages did to the original readers, then even more re-structuring or re-wording must be expected. [Wendland] That is why translation committees have included recognized creative writers with a flair for good English expression, so that the resulting natural English quality can appeal both to the emotions and to the minds of the readers, as any important religious book might be expected to do. [J L Jones, p.15]

But I agree with Carson [Limits, p.211] against Nida who has said that 'translation projects should *begin with stylists* [who enjoy some marginal knowledge of Greek and Hebrew but] *who are competent in the receptor language* and permit the specialists [in Greek and Hebrew] their say *only at the cleaning-up stage.* (my italics and bracketing)

In mockery of the need for stylists even at the final stage, J P Green says: 'When the translators are through, then the entire body of the (NIV) translation is to be given over to stylists. Their duty was to put the Scriptures in the modern style. But of course these persons were not qualified translators, merely stylists. It is presumed that any of the original God-breathed words which did not appeal to the stylists were considered to have no right to

remain the style of the Bible in 20th century English.'
[CLW 1992: 4.2, p.3] Green does not seem to realize that
the Hebrew and the Greek styles are entirely different
from the English style, mainly because the languages are
different! Obviously, no stylist ever looked at the 'translationese' English of his own KJ2 and LTB.

Because more people are likely to hear the version
being read aloud than to read it themselves, attention has
to be paid to the sound of the English so that it does not
happen to convey the wrong meaning. 'Oh Lord' and 'my
God' are nowadays so often used as mere expletives, that
they have been deliberately avoided in CEV Psalms.

Gen. 35:7
RSV: Because there God had revealed himself;
NRS: **Because** *it was there* **that God had revealed himself.**

Mic. 6:12
NJB: For the rich there are steeped in violence and the
citizens there are habitual liars;
REB: **The rich men** *of the city* **are . . .;** *her* **citizens are all
liars.**

Lk. 22:35
RSV: They said, 'Nothing.';
NRS: **They said, 'No, not a thing.'** [Omanson, NRS]

Lk. 7:14
REB: He . . . laid his hand on the bier; NJB: he . . . went up
and touched the bier;
CEV: **Jesus . . . touched the stretcher on which . . .;** TEB: **. . .
went up to the** *coffin* **and touched.**

Ps. 24:1
NAB: The Lord's are the earth and its fullness;
REB: *To the Lord belong* **the earth and.**

Bible versions which seem to have the most natural
English are REB, NJB, LBP, NEB, JB, GOS, MOF, CEV, NIV, GNB;
Barc, jbPh.

10.2 UNNATURAL ENGLISH

If you pick up an unfamiliar Bible in English and start
reading, does it seem to be speaking to you? or to

someone else—of a different century or generation, of a different educational level, or of a different country or denomination? or does it seem not to be speaking on anybody's wavelength?!

Unnatural English can arise from too close imitation of the original grammatical structures:

> who being (Heb. 1:3a); he answering said (Matt. 15:3 JND); O you of little faith (Lk. 12:28 NIV); with desire have I desired (Lk. 22:15 NKJ); blessing I will bless you (Heb. 6:14 NKJ); sons of the bridechamber (Matt. 9:15 KJ2); sons of disobedience; children of the promise; Marriage honorable in all. (Heb. 13:4 DOU); Nazareth of Galilee; purification of sins having achieved (Heb. 1:3 ROT); The things of God knoweth no man, but the Spirit of God (1 Cor. 2:11 KJV) (subject: 'man'!).

Unnatural English can arise from too close imitation of the original words:

> a choinix of wheat for a denarius (AMP); parbar (1 Chr. 26:18 RSV); the heavenlies (Eph. 3:10 JND); baalim (Jer. 9:14 REB); Logos (Jn. 1:1 MOF); life eonian (Jn. 3:16 Conc); the parasceve of the pasch (Jn. 19:14 DOU); against the spirituals of wickedness in the celestials (Eph. 6:12 DOU).

Or words may be used with non-English meanings:

> saints (=God's people, rather than historical personage canonized by the Catholic Church);
>
> justified (=put right with God, rather than defended and excused);
>
> shambles (Jer. 12:3 REB) (=slaughterhouse, rather than confused mess).

Or some words may simply be very unusual:

> eradiated (ROT), actuating (BLE), effulgence, purgation (NEB), outraying (AMP), subsistence (YOU) (all from Heb. 1:3); pygarg (Deut. 14:5 KJV); parturient, caravansaray, parleying, matrix, squab (Lk. 2:5, 7, 19, 23, 24 Conc); keening (Jer. 9:17 REB) (for wailing); do your devoir (Ex. 32:29 BLE) (for be dedicated); deodand (Jos. 6–7 BLE) (for devoted); legist (Lk. 11:52 BLE) (for lawyer).

Abnormal collocations of words may strike the reader as merely odd:

reproduction of his essence (Wuest), Emblem of His assumption (Conc), figure of his substance (CHA), the saying of his might, the all things (YOU), the word of his power (all from Heb. 1:3); fruit of his loins (Acts 2:30 KJ2); molten sea (RSV); put the branch to the nose (NIV); their destruction has not been sleeping (2 Pet. 2:3 NIV); crippled by a spirit (Lk. 13:11 NIV); he had no union with her (Matt. 1:25 NIV); heap coals of fire on his head (Rom. 12:20 KJV, RAV); life of the ages (Weym); system of things (NWT) for age; little-faiths (Lk. 12:28 BLE); why doesn't the Holy One of Israel's design hurry up and come true . . .? (Isa. 5:19 NJB).

Or may introduce some irreverent amusement:

thy right hand causeth thee to stumble (Matt. 5:29 RV); straitened in your own bowels (2 Cor. 6:12 KJV); grease your head (Matt. 6:17 NWT); folding the sheep (Gen. 29:7 NEB), penning the sheep (REB), loose livers (1 Cor. 5:9 NEB); run a bootless race (Phil. 2:16 BLE); the spiritual rock-mass (1 Cor. 10:4 NWT); stand in the way of sinners (Ps. 1:1 NIV) (not: obstruct); right in his eyes (Ex. 15:26 REB); died to sin (Rom. 6:2) (not very anxious to); have it as you have faith for (Matt. 9:29 BLE); they that are after the flesh (Rom. 8:5) (not carnivores); fell on his neck (Lk. 15:20 KJV) (not headlong); took his journey into a far country (Lk. 15:13 RSV); one of his students . . . was lying in Jesus' lap (Jn. 13:23 Gaus) [Bratcher, Unvarnished]; putting on . . . the hope of being delivered as a helmet (1 Thess. 5:8 Stern); 'It is kindness that I (the Lord) want,' (Matt. 9:13 GNB).

Expanded translations heap up synonyms of the more important words, thereby grossly overloading the English:

Whom He appointed Heir and lawful Owner of all things, also by and through Whom He created the worlds and the reaches of space and the ages of time—[that is] He made, produced, built, operated, and arranged them in order. (Heb. 1:2 AMP, cf. also Matt. 5.)

Simplified translations have to use constant circumlocutions to replace technical terms excluded from their basic vocabulary of about 1000 words:

'things God gives you to fight with' for 'armor';
'special box that held the Old Way of Worship' for 'Ark of the Covenant';

'workman who is owned by someone' for 'slave' (all Ledyard).

Because BBE has far more nouns than verbs in its 850-word vocabulary, it is forced into such circumlocutions even for common words:

'give ear' for 'listen'; 'have knowledge' for 'know'; 'are dear to' for 'love'.

When careful attention is paid to the nuances of the Greek tenses, the English tends to become too heavy:

If you do get angry, you must stop sinning in your anger. Do not ever let the sun go down on your anger; stop giving the devil a chance. The man who used to steal must now stop stealing; rather he must keep on working and toiling with his own hands at some honest vocation, so as to have something to contribute to the needy. (Eph. 4:26–28 cbWi)

Word-for-word translations of the New Testament tend to have sentences which are far longer than is normal in English. For example, 2 Pet. 2:4–9 is one sentence in NIV, as is Heb. 1:1–4 in DOU, NKJ; see also Eph. 1:3–14; Rom. 1:1–4; 2:14–21; Col. 1:9–20.

In Old Testament narrative, such translations may start almost every clause with 'and', quite contrary to normal adult English usage.

Simplified translations produce a similar 'breathless' effect with their very short sentences, though without conjunctions:

He spoke through the early preachers. But in these last days He has spoken to us through His Son. God gave His Son everything. It was by His Son that God made the world. The Son shines with the shining greatness of the Father. The Son is as God is in every way. (Heb. 1:1–3 Ledy)

While some Bible versions have only a few abnormal words and expressions, others (like AMP; Conc; LTB, KJ2, NWT, YOU) are full of them and so can be said to have the most unnatural English.

10.3 DIVERSITY OF STYLES

Open any English translation of the Bible and observe whether Psalms and Acts look the same at first glance.

Before the nineteenth century, no distinction at all was made between poetry and prose in the printed format (KJV, etc); but some twentieth-century translations equally fail to distinguish them (KJ2, LBP, AMP, LAM, KNO, BBE).

Some print only Psalms and Proverbs as poetry (BLE, NBV, NWT, RV). But, since nearly half of the Old Testament is actually poetry in Hebrew, most modern translations reflect this fact by additionally printing as poetry most of the Prophets, Job, Lamentations, as well as the songs of Miriam, Deborah, etc. (NIV, RAV, GNB, CEV, TEB, REB, NRS, NAS, etc). NAB1 (not 2) and NJB further recognize poetical forms in the New Testament, especially in John and 1 John; similarly, MOF, Barc in Matthew and Luke.

Where poetry is printed as such in the appropriate places in a Bible version, not only is the original being faithfully represented, but the reader's understanding is also facilitated.

Poetry itself is found in different styles: lyrical, liturgical, prophetic, didactic, etc. Biblical prose also is diverse, with history in Kings, prophecy in Isaiah, law in Leviticus, a letter like Titus, narrative and dialogue and descriptions in the Gospels and Acts; we also find argumentation and exhortation in the NT letters.

Just as the Bible in its 66 books with many diferent authors was not written in a single style throughout, so an English translation of it should equally not be in a single style throughout, if it is faithfully to represent the original. Different individuals on a translation panel should therefore translate different books of the Bible with their individual styles; and editorial committees, reviewing their work, should not be so heavy-handed as to insist on stylistic uniformity.

One-man translations inevitably tend to have one style throughout (JND, BLE, KJ2), as do expanded translations (AMP) and simplified ones (BBE, Ledy, Cres).

10.4   FIGURATIVE EXPRESSIONS

The poetical parts should not only be printed as such, they should also sound as far as possible like natural

English poetry, with, for example, a metrical beat for each line, sound symbolism, perhaps even rhyme. One would also expect striking imagery and figurative expressions which go beyond ordinary everyday grammatical patterns and word collocations.

Knox, however, has gone too far in his attempt to make poetical language different from normal:

'Way-marks leave behind thee, sad trophies be raising as thou goest, to put thee in mind of the straight road thou hast trodden. Return thou must, poor Israel, return thou must to these, thy own cities; fickle maid, dally no longer.' (Jer. 31:21–2)

Figures of speech should preferably be retained in the translation provided that their original meaning is perfectly understood. But translators have varied in their estimate of what figures of speech can be translated word-for-word and still retain the original meaning:

Jas 1.15
NRS: **when that desire has conceived, it gives birth to sin, and that sin, when it is fully grown, gives birth to death;**
TEB: This desire causes sin. Then the sin grows and brings death.

Isa. 52:1
* 'clothe strength-your'
NJB: **clothe yourself in strength;** REB, NRS: **put on your strength;**
TEB: become strong

Various OT contexts
he rested with his fathers
NRS: **he slept with his ancestors;**
TEB: he died.

Jn. 8:31
NJB: **if you make my word your home;**
CEV: if you keep on obeying what I have said

Various OT contexts
*the Virgin Daughter of Zion
TEB: the people of Jerusalem.

Where an original figure of speech would not be

understood if translated word-for-word, it is best if it can be replaced by an equivalent English figure:

Amos 2:7
RSV, NRS: trample the head of the poor;
jbP: grind the faces of the poor

Isa. 3:16
RSV, NRS: with outstretched necks;
jbP: with noses in the air [Fee & Stuart, p.38].

2 Jn. 12
*mouth to mouth
RAV, NAB, REB: **face to face;**
CEV, NJB: in person; GNB: personally

If too many original figures of speech have had to be changed in order to preserve the original meaning, it may be desirable to introduce figures in the translation where there was no figure in the original; for example, in Matt. 27:44, the literal 'he reproached him' becomes 'he cast the same in his teeth' (KJV) [Clark, Problems 2, p.9]

Exclamations may be translated literally, or figures may be introduced; in the first case below, the Elizabethan oath is suitable, but hardly in the second case:

2 Sam. 18:33
*'Who will grant my death, I instead of you?'
NRS, REB: Would (that) I had died instead of you!;
KJV, RV, JND: **Would God I had died! . . . .**

Rom. 6:2
* 'May it not happen!'
NRS: **By no means!** REB: **Certainly not!;** CEV: **No, we should not!;** JND: **Far be the thought!;**
KJV, RV: God forbid!.

SUMMARY

It has been mainly from more modern versions of the Bible that the examples of unnatural English expressions have been drawn. In some of these versions (see the end of 8.3), unnatural expressions are common; while in others, they are exceptional (see the end of 8.2).

Naturalness is important because it permeates every line of a translation. Its readers or hearers can then receive a similar impact as the original receivers, and so have the opportunity of making equivalent responses to the Bible message. This was the avowed aim of dynamically-equivalent translations.

Of course, the naturalness, or even the beauty, of the English expression must not be at the expense of translating the full original meaning, which must have absolute priority. Otherwise, it would be like having thick decorative icing on a poor-quality cake! [Nida, Quality]

11

The English of today or of yesterday?

11.1 OF TODAY OR OF YESTERDAY?

In addition to our being speakers and readers of the English language, another thing you and I have in common is that we belong to the late twentieth century. So the Bible versions which we use today should not be weighted down with relics of yesterday's English—or indeed that of the day before yesterday! According to Campbell [Foster, p.9], at least every two hundred years the Bible should be translated again to keep it in the living language of the people; though a period of one hundred years, when three generations have passed, might be more appropriate. No modern translator of the Bible into an African or other language would ever think of translating into a nineteenth or seventeenth-century form of that language if the people are meant to understand and respond to the Bible message. Such people, who may never have heard the gospel before, are not so different from the largely post-Christian English-speaking world of today.

Very early English translations (like COV, GRT, BIS) were all printed in the impressive 'black letter' font (similar to the German script recently superseded). It was GEN and DOU which pioneered the modern practice of printing in roman letters. In the eighteenth century, all noun initials were capitalized (as still in modern German); this is found in Will and PUR: 'Things', 'Word', 'Cleansing', 'Sins' (from Heb. 1:3).

Bible translations up to the seventeenth century all used what seems to us as archaic spellings. From Heb. 1:1–3 mostly (modern spellings in parentheses):

> al (all), awne (own), beyng (being), bi (by), brightnes, glorie, hee (he), lunatick, pourged, purgacioun, schynynge (shining), substaunce, synnes (sins), vppe (up), thingis, whanne (one), woord (word), ymage (image).

Of these older translations, most have never been reprinted for general use, except KJV whose archaic spellings have been gradually modernized over the centuries.

However, KJV still has all the archaic grammatical endings and forms:

> hath, walkedst, is come, holpen (helped), unwashen, would fain, must needs, a-fishing, how that, twain, to you-ward, an hungred, Father which, whosoever, howbeit, lest, peradventure, aforetime, yea, nay.

The Andersons (p.4–5) consider that the singular/plural distinction between 'thou' and 'ye' found in KJV (eg. 1 Cor. 3:17: 'which temple ye are') must be continued in modern Bible translations in order 'to avoid the twentieth-century individualism so rampant in the Church today—an individualism perpetuated by the (NIV)'s lack of differentiation between singular and plural forms in (the above verse)'. The 'fault', of course, lies not in NIV, but in the English language!

Incredibly, Paisley (p.45) argues that the KJV 'like unto me' (Deut. 18:15) is better than the REB 'like me', which is the normal translation of the Hebrew original. He also thinks (p.15–17) that, in John 1 etc., 'only begotten' (KJV) implies deity, while 'only' (which is normal English for this meaning) does not!

Paisley and those who think like him should realize that the English language has changed over the centuries, and should not impute heresy, or worse, to those who translate into normal modern English.

Most of the archaic forms quoted above may be quite understandable especially to the better educated; but a version like KJV is so heavily loaded with them that the overall archaic atmosphere may prove rather suffocating. And most modern versions also have some archaisms:

REB: betimes (Jer. 21:12); putting . . . to the proof (Ps. 26:2).

The Trinitarian Bible Society offers a 'Daily Reading Scheme' for reading through the Bible in two years. But, at the beginning of the booklet, is a list of 600 so-called 'Bible words' (from KJV) requiring explanation for the modern reader—which seems to be an excellent reason for not using KJV when following the reading scheme!

Some of these KJV words and expressions actually mean nothing to the modern reader:

behooved, chode, bewrayeth (not betrayeth), strawed, ambassage, fuller, marish, chambering, murrain (plague) (Ex. 9:3), scall (itch; Lev. 13:30), froward (1 Pet. 2:18). Wist ye not? (Lk. 2:49); We do you to wit (2 Cor. 8:1) (we must tell you REB); Jacob sod pottage (Gen. 25:29; was preparing broth REB).

Other KJV words and expressions suggest the wrong meaning, not to its original readers, but to the modern reader:

occurrent (misfortune) (1 Ki. 5:4), flagons (raisins) (Cant. 2:5), round tires like the moon (crescent ornaments) (Isa. 3:18), stomacher (waistband), virtue (power), charger (plate), meat (food), husbandman (farmer), charity (love), wealth (well-being), reins (kidneys, heart), conversation (conduct) (1 Pet. 2:12), jangling (discussion) (1 Tim. 1:6), audience (hearing), abroad (outside), quick (alive), stout (brave), outlandish (foreign) (Neh. 13:26); dumb RSV (silent NRS) (Ps. 39:9), translate (remove), scrabble (collect), offend (cause to sin), advertise (advise), communicate (share), let (hinder), fine (refine) (Job 28:1). [Giese; Ellington]

Respecting persons (favoritism) (Deut. 1:17; Acts 10:34); the host was secure (Jdg. 8:11; the army was off its guard RSV, NRS); I prevented the dawning of the morning (Ps.

119:147; before dawn REB); we which are ... shall not prevent them which ... (1 Thess. 4:15; have advantage over REB); throughly furnished (well-prepared) (2 Tim. 3:17); minister (attendant REB) (Lk. 4:20); purchase a good degree (gain a good standing) (1 Tim. 3:13); sick of the palsy (Mk. 2:10) (not fed up with being ill); the bowels of the saints are refreshed (Phlm. 7; set the hearts of God's ... people at rest NJB).

REB: of myself /I reck nothing (Job 9:21; I am no longer sure NJB).

In 'Study to shew thyself approved unto God' (2 Tim. 2:15), 'study' has nothing to do with Bible study, but rather with diligence: 'do your best' (JND, NIV). Likewise, 'study to be quiet' (1 Thess. 4:11) means 'make a point of living quietly' (NJB).

The sixteenth-century (rather than seventeenth-century) archaism of KJV was deliberately continued till the end of the nineteenth century by translations like RV, JND, YOU, while twentieth-century revisions in the KJV tradition tend to perpetuate old-fashioned words and expressions. One could certainly argue that Judges 5, Job, parts of Isaiah, and some other Old Testament passages, could be translated into somewhat archaic English because they had an archaic ring to them even in the original Hebrew. Or even the whole of the OT could be in an older form of English than the New Testament (cf. Knox); or OT quotations in the NT could be in older English, as some versions (eg. Weymouth, Phillips) have done.

Though some modern versions have used 'you' for singular and plural throughout, they have used 'thou' when addressing God (NAS, NEB, NBV, RSV, MOF, GOS). But the most fully up-to-date English, without any 'thou' at all, can be found in NIV, GNB, BLE, LBP, NAB, NJB, NWT, BBE, REB, CEV, TEB, NRS.

Although we have quoted innumerable examples of archaic words from KJV, we are not blaming the KJV translators in the slightest! They are not responsible for the fact that the English language has changed. We rather have a responsibility to seek out that original meaning which the KJV translators well expressed in the English of their generation.

'One sometimes gets the impression that certain objections to modern versions of the Bible may be due to the *starkness with which they thrust the plain sense on the reader,* whereas the more archaic idiom of older versions carries a kind 'distance' with it.' [Bruce, What does it mean?; my italics)

The Andersons, incredibly, complain that the NIV 'uses *detailed language*—language inappropriate for this paper and certainly out of place in a Book whose Author desires the transforming of the mind to His standards. It is doubtful that the *descriptive language* used in the (NIV), particularly that in Ezekiel 23, would be used even in the daily newspaper. It could certainly not be read to a child, and would only cause the mind of an unbeliever to stray away from the message of the Scriptures. Modernising the Bible is one thing; *vulgarising* it is uncalled for.' [p.14 my italics] Here, their prudishness has taken them so far as to complain, not of the language of the NIV or any other modern version, but rather of what God has clearly put into his Word, whether they like it or not!

The young people of a congregation which normally uses an archaic version in public may get used to hearing frequent explanations and corrections of the old words; cg 'conversation' really means 'conduct'; or 'charity' does not mean 'charity' but 'love'. But this tends to erode their whole-hearted acceptance of God's words in the Bible.

In any case, letting ('allowing' not 'preventing'!) God's word be publicly read in anything but twentieth-century English is surely a betrayal of God's commission to us as Christians to preach the gospel to our world.

11.2 SEXUALLY-BIASED EXPRESSIONS

Very rarely has any woman produced, or even participated in, any translation of the Bible. Exceptions are Julia Smith (1876), Spurrell (OT 1885), Mrs Hooke (participated in BBE), participants in NRS, and Montgomery (Centenary NT).

Hints of a female hand in Montgomery may perhaps be found in 'minister' (Rom. 16:1); 'deaconess' (1 Tim. 3:11); the female name 'Junia' (Rom. 16:7); a quoted opinion on women speaking in church (1 Cor. 14:34–6) [Bullard].

GNB (cf REB) correctly has 'many women' (Ps. 68:11) to translate a Hebrew feminine participle, rather than 'a great army' (TEB).

Nowadays people have become more sensitive to sexual bias in the English language. Consequently, many modern versions have tried to avoid expressions which are biased in favour of men, where the original evidently refers to both sexes.

The traditional 'man' (collective) or 'men' can be translated as 'humanity', 'human beings' or 'the human race' (some object to 'mankind'!) or 'people' (* indicates the original literal word):

> Gen. 1:26
> *adam
> KJV NJB NIV: man; LBP: a man;
> NRS: **humankind;** GNB REB TEB: **human beings.**
>
> Isa. 40:6
> KJV, KJ2: *flesh; NIV: men; LBP: man;
> GNB1/2: **mankind / human beings;** NJB: **humanity;** NRS, TEB: **people;** REB: **mortals.**
>
> Matt. 5:16
> NIV, RAV: men;
> NRS, CEV: **others;** GNB, NJB: ***people;** TEB: **other people;** REB: your fellows.
>
> Jn. 12:32
> RSV, NIV: *all men;
> RAV: all peoples; NRS, TEB, NJB: **all people;** REB, CEV: **everyone.**
>
> 2 Tim. 3:17
> *person
> KJV: man of God;
> NJB: **someone dedicated to God;** CEV: **God's servant.**

'The man who' or 'he who' can be translated as 'those who' or 'all who', rather than 'whoever' or 'anyone who'

(NAB2) because the latter has to continue with 'he, him, his':

Ps. 1:1–3
KJV, KJ2, RAV, NIV: the *man that/who; REB: the one who . . . his . . . he . . .; TEB: the person who . . . he . . . he; NJB: anyone . . . such a one; **GNB, NRS: those who . . . they . . . .**

Jas. 4:17
KJV: him . . . him; RSV: *whoever . . . him; TEB, GNB1: a person . . . he; BLE/KJ2: one / anyone . . . his/him; **REB, NRS, NIV: anyone; NJB: everyone; GNB2: we . . . we . . . we . . . we; CEV: you . . . you . . . you.**

The NT term of address, 'brethren', 'brothers', has been translated as 'friends' (REB, GNB2–US), which seems to be too weak in meaning; 'brothers and sisters' (GNB2-UK) is better, though clumsy, if not 'fellow-believers':

Gal. 3:15; 6:1, 18
KJV: brethren; NEB, TEB, KJ2, GNB1, NJB, NIV, NAB1: brothers; REB, GNB2-US, CEV: friends; **NRS: brothers and sisters / friends; GNB2-UK: brothers and sisters.**

Jas. 1:9
KJ2, NJB, NIV: brother . . .; TEB: a believer . . . (he . . . him . . .); REB: the church member . . . (his . . .); **NRS: believer; GNB: Christians . . . Christians . . .; CEV: any of God's people . . . them** [Bratcher, REB].

The modern versions that have been most serious about removing unnecessary sexual bias from the English are NRS, CEV, GNB2; while others, like KJ2, RAV, NAS, NWT, Cass, and all pre-1960 versions, seem unaware of the problem.

12

At whose level of English is it readable?

In the previous chapters we have considered whether the English of the Bible versions is adequate under two headings, with clear conclusions: the English should be as natural and as up-to-date as possible, and these conclusions must apply to every reader of English today.

12.1 WHAT IS 'READABILITY'?

If a message is entirely 'predictable' from one word or sentence to the next, you lose interest and soon give up listening or reading. Think of the elderly person who makes the same predictable remarks to visitors, or repeats the same old stories or complaints. Or think of a children's story being read aloud by a parent. From the point of view of the visitors or of the parent, there is a very high level of 'predictability'—they know what is coming next!

In contrast, a fresh student, on attending lectures in a new subject by a learned professor, might have the opposite experience: what he hears is so 'unpredictable' from one sentence to the next that he might easily get lost. The lectures are too much for him to swallow; the information load is too heavy.

Neither extreme 'predictability' or extreme 'unpredictability' is normal or desirable in language. [Wonderly, ch. 17; Nida & Taber, ch. 6] Rather, in order to sustain interest, a piece of writing should be about 50% 'predictable' (or redundant, in the Information Theory sense). It is this 50% level which is termed 'readable', a mean between extremes.

Readability is not an inherent property of Bible translations (or of any other written material), but is relative to the intended readers' capacity. Therefore, a version which is readable to the poorly-educated church member is far from readable to the well-educated new convert; and vice versa!

In other words, groups of people just differ from each other in various ways, and so may legitimately require different versions if they are to receive God's message in the Bible with its full impact, for them to make an appropriate response, equivalent to that made by the original readers of the original message. This is the primary goal of 'dynamic equivalence' translation. It involves adjusting the level of English expression to suit different capacities of intended readers; but it must not involve changing the original message in a misguided effort to 'transculturate' it into the culture of these readers. [Carson, Limits]

In a survey of the understandability (readability) of two Bible versions among junior secondary-modern school pupils, it was deduced from the scores that none would read KJV on their own; and two-thirds would give up reading KJV if not compelled; whereas about one-seventh would read GNB on their own; and only one-fifth would give up if not compelled. [Rye]

Another survey of readability based on three Bible passages gave the following results, from most to least difficult: KJV, RSV, NEB, LBP, NIV, GNB.

Yet another survey found that Cressman and Ledyard were barely two-thirds understandable to 11–12-year-olds; while GNB and Laubach were even less so to 14–15-year-olds. [Sjölander & Rye]—which makes nonsense of the suggestion that at age 11 GNB should be replaced by RSV!

More informally, army men found KJV and RSV incomprehensible, in contrast to GNB and JBP, according to J L

Jones (p.42); these were no doubt all native speakers of English.

12.2   LITERARY OR COLLOQUIAL LEVELS?

University graduates, or those who have specialized in literature, or those who have become professional writers, may admire Elizabethan classics of English literature, like Shakespeare and the KJV Bible. Some have even complained that modern Bible translations have been altering the KJV English, while no one would ever think of rewriting Shakespeare! According to T S Eliot: 'Those who talk of the Bible as a "monument of English prose" are merely admiring it as a monument over the grave of Christianity.' [Bratcher, Hargreaves]

If one starts with that premise, then one may well complain (with Newell) that less literary translations appear to trivialise the language, to debase literary taste, and belong to a low educative level.

Literary extravagance was carried to the extreme in the eighteenth-century Harwood:

O Sir! What a delectable residence we might establish here. (Lk. 9:33) [Foster, p.42]

But more recently, fairly high-level literary translations include NEB/REB, (N)JB, KNO, MOF, FEN; Cass, Scho, Latt, West, JPSA.

NEB has the following words:

purgation, effulgence, ague, miscreant, descry, bedizened, contumely, ministrant, parricide, felicity, put out of countenance.

KNO has:

On all nations the Lord will be avenged, never an armed host but must feel the blow, forfeit, all of them, and doomed to perish. (Isa. 34:2)

Most of the older versions can also be taken as literary, formal and dignified, suitable for use in church services.

These are no doubt the 'ecclesiastical language' translations advocated by van Bruggen for non-Christians to avoid building a 'barrier between the church and evangelism' (p.140). Such people are expected to adopt the church's in-group language (and no doubt other characteristics) in order to become Christians!

Because of my own education in languages up to university level, I can readily cope with the above-noted literary Bible versions. But literary appreciation is not well developed in most people, even educated people; and Christians should by no means feel obliged to develop their literary sensibilities in order to read the Bible.

At the opposite extreme from literary translations are colloquial, conversational, translations of the Bible like Peterson and LBP. But colloquial language might include slang and other substandard features which would make it unsuitable for public worship.

LBP has:

yanking, act big, shoo away; a population explosion (Gen. 6:1); a cocky brat (1 Sam. 17:28).

jbPh has:

To hell with you and your money! (Acts 8:20).

CEV has:

you showoffs! (Matt. 22:18)

12.3 COMMON LANGUAGE LEVEL

In Old Testament times 'Ezra read plainly from the book of the law of God, interpreting it so that all could understand what was said.' (Neh. 8:8 NAB). Even then, the classical Hebrew was not well understood; and so right down to Jesus' time it was normally interpreted into Aramaic during synagogue Bible readings. 'With many stories like these Jesus was telling them the message— *but only as much as they were able to understand*' (Mk. 4:33 Simp, my italics)

Moreover, the New Testament was never written in classical, literary Greek, but rather in the *koine* (common) Greek used every day in the eastern Mediterranean, rather like English is used today as a *lingua franca* throughout the world.

In the fourteenth and sixteenth centuries, first Wyclif and then Tyndale risked their lives to translate the Bible from the 'ecclesiastical Latin' Vulgate into English, the language of the people. Erasmus, the great editor of the Greek NT, was anxious that the Bible be read by all kinds of unlearned people, even women, Scots, Irish, Turks, Saracens, farm-workers, weavers, travellers!

Nowadays, many adults, who finished their compulsory schooling around the ages of fifteen or sixteen, maintain a reading age of that level, or even lower if they do not habitually read books. Although the more sensational popular newspapers and magazines tend towards the colloquial, the less sensational ones, including local papers, may be written around that basic or common level of English. Therefore, such papers can be readily understood, not only by those for whom they are intended, but also by those who have gone higher up the educational ladder, even though the latter may feel such language is rather low for them!

This level of language can then be said to be 'common' to everyone. If you take away the higher features of literary language and the lower features of colloquial language, you find that these two levels of language have a considerable overlap—in common. Similarly, there is a considerable overlap between the language of Christians and of non-Christians. Common language has grammar and vocabulary 'which no user of English would disdain to use, which no native speaker of English would fail to understand, and which those who have learned English as a second language would find easily comprehensible.' [GNB Translation Principles; Nida, Good News ch. 11, Quality; Carson, Limits; J L Jones, p.36; Loewen, Who]

Such common language is characterized by shorter, simpler sentences, rather than complex ones with subordinate clauses (compare Eph. 1:3–14 in KJV, NIV, GNB); avoidance of confusion if it is heard, rather than read (not: As I was returning from Paddan, to my sorrow Rachel died. (Gen. 48:7 NIV)); actions, processes, and states expressed by verbs with subjects and objects, rather than by abstract nouns ('we are saved, he saved us' instead of 'our salvation'); simpler words ('stay, carry, service' instead of 'remain, bear, ministry') including theological terms (like 'change your ways' replacing 'repent').

Theological terms, which hardly number more than fifty in all, are actually shorthand expressions for theological experience, known to Christians as a sort of 'church jargon', but not to others. [Wonderly, 5.8] Some feel that the terms themselves are absolutely sacrosanct, and so cannot be expressed otherwise. But is meaning actually lost or gained if the term 'reconciled' becomes 'changed . . . from enemies into his friends', and 'reconciliation' becomes 'making others his friends also' (2 Cor. 5:18 GNB)?

Because most Bible translators have themselves been very highly educated in academic subjects, it is they who may find it most difficult to come down from their higher language level to that of ordinary everyday speech! [Loewen, Who; Clark, Culture]

The only Bible versions which are explicitly said to be in common English are GNB and CEV. CEV, however, has, in Matt. 22 alone, words like banquet, furious, grit their teeth, footstool, commandment.

Tran is also simple, direct and uncomplicated in language. And other versions are claimed to be 'everyday' (TEB), 'in the language of today' (BEC), 'simple English' (Simp), 'simplified, in plain English—for today's reader' (Norlie), 'in plain English' (ckWi), 'in the language of the people' (cbWi), or for young people (jbPH), and so they may also tend to be in common language.

Objections have been raised, even to NIV, on the grounds that it is not *foreign* or *classical* enough to properly reveal the ancient culture of the Jews. Compared with the unusual wording of KJV or ASV, NIV is also '*less easily memorized* and less easily "hidden in the heart" as God would have it to be . . . The NIV is so easy to read that it is often read as one might read a newspaper, *quickly and*

with little comprehension. An advantage of greater difficulty in reading is that one is more apt to read slowly
and pick up nuances and meanings hidden from the
rapid reader . . . While it is true that the NIV requires less
adult supervision and guidance when being read, *it also
deprives the parent of opportunities of spiritual interaction,* opportunities that may never come again.' [Ander-
sons, pp.5–6, 2; my italics]

If your religion affects the whole of your life, then its
language should be that of everyday life; and all the more
so, if you try to reach out and tell the gospel to outsiders
who have had little contact with real Christianity.

12.4 SIMPLIFIED

If you have to get across to someone a message which is
strange and 'unpredictable', then you could repeat it, as
in Acts 10 where God's unexpected message to Peter had
to come three times. Or terms like 'God, Word, light,
world, grace' could be repeated in clusters as in Jn. 1:1–
18 (cf. 1 Jn.) [Chow]. Or background details can be filled
in, as in Jn. 4:8 where John explains why Jesus was alone
and 4:9 why the woman was surprised at Jesus' request.
If all these methods of improving understandability
were needed for the receivers of the original Bible
messages, how much more must similar methods be
followed for the benefit of the receivers of Bible translations! [Beekman, Idiomatic; Lode]
This is especially true for those who are trying to learn
the English language, either as a mother tongue, or as a
second language after their own, or as a completely
foreign language. All such people are in a transitional
stage, through which most of them will soon pass and
become more proficient in English. Meanwhile, they may
use translations which have been specially simplified by
restricting the length, and so the complexity, of sentences;
by restricting the total vocabulary used (to 850 words BBE,
to 1500 ckWi, to 850 Ledy); by replacing pronouns with

nouns where necessary; by repeating the end of one sentence at the beginning of the next (especially ETR, also called English Version for the Deaf).

'Long ago, God talked to our fathers through the prophets. He talked in many parts and in many ways. In these last days, he talked to us through his Son. God caused him to be the one to whom he would give all things. God also made the world by this Son.' (Heb. 1:1–2 Cres)

Laubach, a world literacy expert, produced The Inspired Letters of Paul. The United Bible Societies are also producing New Reader Selections in various languages.

But simplified translations cannot be recommended for general adult use.

12.5 'CRIB' OR 'GLOSS'

If you belong to that small group of serious students of the Bible who are trying to learn the Hebrew or Greek languages, then you will appreciate the value especially of an interlinear translation, or a more or less 'crib' or 'gloss' translation, in which every word has its exact English counterpart. Examples of the latter are KJ2, NWT, YOU, JND, RV, DOU; Conc.

But the more suitable a translation is for the Hebrew/ Greek learner, the less suitable it is likely to be for ordinary unlearned people.

SUMMARY

The only language that is appropriate for the Bible for today's reader is an English which is perfectly normal and natural, and reflects the original diversity of poetic and prose styles. Moreover, the English must be entirely up-to-date and without the older sexual bias.

Although neither denominational nor national origin should be evident in a version, some people of a higher educational level may well be more at ease with a relatively literary Bible translation. But they can equally well understand a common-language version also, so that such a version can be recommended for everyone.

But, it should always be remembered that: 'Even though the vocabulary and grammatical patterns of a Bible translation may be quite readable, yet the reader may baulk at the meaning which God is trying to convey in his word, or he may baulk at believing that meaning and acting on his belief; but that is outside the province of the translator per se.' [L. Hohulin, pp.22–4, my plain type]

Is It Well Presented?

13

Is it clear enough?

Chapters 5–9 examined the original meaning which is to be translated as faithfully as possible. Chapters 10–12 examined the nature of the English expression. In this chapter and the next two, we shall look at how Bible translations are presented.

This chapter deals with the clarity or intelligibility of translations. To some extent we have dealt with this in chapters 8–9 where it was pointed out that too close imitation of the original wording of long sentences and of phrases may lead to obscurity in the translation; for example:

> Yet, before the twins were born or had done anything good or bad—in order that God's purpose in election might stand: not by works but by him who calls—she was told, 'The older will serve the younger.' (Rom. 9:11–12 NIV); Nazareth of Galilee; holy of holies; the gospel of the uncircumcision (Gal. 2:7); obedience of faith (Rom. 1:5); faith of Christ (Gal. 2:16).

All of these can be clarified by discovering the full meaning and then translating it faithfully into natural English.

13.1 DO THE PRONOUNS REFER CLEARLY?

It is very easy for Bible translators who are well versed in the teaching of the Bible to fail to make clear in their

Bible translation the exact references of third-person
pronouns. Readers of the translation should not have to
back-track to find these references, and listeners to a
public Bible reading cannot do so. In each case below,
the English equivalents given in **bold** type are preferred
to the equivalents in plain type.

Gen. 6:5
NJB: Yahweh saw that human wickedness was great on
earth and that *his* heart contrived nothing but wicked
schemes . . .;
REB: **When the Lord saw how great was the wickedness of
human beings on earth, and their every thought and inclin-
ation were always wicked.**

Jdg. 3:6
RSV: and *they* took *their* daughters to *themselves* for wives,
and *their* own daughters *they* gave to *their* sons; and *they*
served *their* gods;
GNB: **They intermarried with them and worshipped their
gods.**

1 Sam. 15:2
NAS: I will punish Amalek for what *he* did to Israel, how
he set *himself* against *him* on the way while *he* was coming
up from Egypt;
NRS: **I will punish the Amalekites for what they did in
opposing the Israelites when they came up out of Egypt.**

1 Chr. 7:21
NAS: Ez. and El. whom the men of Gath . . . killed because
they came down to take *their* livestock;
GNB: **who were killed when they tried to steal the cattle
belonging to . . . of Gath.**

2 Chr. 17:1
NJB: When *his* son Jehoshaphat succeeded *him*, *he* made
himself stronger against Israel;
JB: **His son Jehoshaphat succeeded him and consolidated
his power over Israel.**

Ps. 119:98
NIV: Your commands make me wiser than my enemies, for
they are ever with me;
NRS: **Your commandment makes me wiser than my enemies,
for it is always with me.**

Heb. 1:3
NAS (NWT, LAM): and He is the radiance of His glory and the exact representation of His nature; BLE (KJV, RV, JND, Wues): who, being beam of his glory and imprint of his essence;
NIV (REB, NAB1, LBP, ETR, jbPh): **The Son is the radiance of God's glory** ...

NIV(GNB): sustaining all things by his powerful word;
Ledy (ETR): It is the Son Who holds up the whole world by the power of His Word.

NIV: After he had provided purification for sins;
ETR (Ledy): **The Son made people clean from their sins.**

Matt. 12:9–10
NRS: He left that place and entered their synagogue; a man was there with a withered hand, and they asked him, 'Is it lawful to cure on the sabbath?';
REB: **He went on** " " " **A man was there with** " " " , **and they asked Jesus,** ... [Newman, Readability]

Matt. 17:24, 25
NRS: When they reached Capernaum, the collectors of the temple tax ... And when he came home, Jesus spoke of it first, [Omanson, NRS];
GNB: **When Jesus and his disciples came to Capernaum, the collectors ... When Peter went into the house, Jesus spoke up first.**

Lk. 19:4
REB: So he ran on ahead and climbed a ... tree in order to see him, for he was to pass that way;
NJB: **he ... climbed a ... tree to catch a glimpse of Jesus who was to pass that way.**

Jn. 12:41
NRS: Isaiah said this because he saw his glory and spoke about him. ... many ... believed in him;
GNB: **Isaiah said this because he saw Jesus' glory and spoke about him. ... many ... believed in Jesus** [Newman, New way].

2 Cor. 5:21
KJV: He hath made him to be sin for us, who knew no sin;
NRS: For our sake he made him to be sin, who knew no sin;

REB: **Christ was innocent of sin, and yet for our sake God made him one with human sinfulness.**

1 *Thess. 2:16*
NRS: by hindering us from speaking to the Gentiles so that *they* may be saved. Thus *they* have constantly been filling up the measure of *their* sins;
CEV: **They keep us from speaking his message to the Gentiles and from leading them to be saved. The Jews have always gone too far with their sins.**

In general, it is the less word-for-word and more modern versions that are likely to notice and avoid such problems of obscure pronoun reference.

13.2 ARE CERTAIN PRONOUNS MADE PROMINENT?

The best-known introduction to emphatic statements in the New Testament is Jesus' words:

'Amen, amen, I say to you' (NAB2), 'Verily, verily, I say unto you' (KJV), 'Truly, truly, I tell you' (NRS).

However, we are going to start our discussion of prominence on a much smaller scale. Both in Hebrew and in Greek, subject pronouns normally formed one word with the verb; but they could also be expressed separately for prominence or emphasis. Most English translations ignore this; but some do indicate such separate pronouns by typographical devices.

Below, the upper sets of examples ignore the emphasis, while the lower sets make some attempt to indicate it, whether by ´ or by ‖. . .‖, or by *italics*, or by **bold**, which last is the most readily visible and understandable.

Mk. 9:28
REB: Why could we not drive it out?
GNB: Why couldn't we drive the spirit out?
Conc: Wherefore could we´ not cast it out?
Roth: |Why| were ‖we‖ not able to cast it out?
JND: Wherefore could not *we* cast him out?
Simp: Why were **we** not able to throw out the . . . ?

Jn. 14:6
REB: I am the way, the truth, and the life.
jbP2: I myself am the way,' . . .
JND: I am the way, and the truth, and the life.
Simp: I am the way and the truth and the life!

Matt. 3:14
NRS: I need to be baptized by you, and do you come to me?
REB: 'Do you come to me?' he said. 'It is I who need to be baptized by you.'
Roth: |I| have |need| ‖by thee‖ to be immersed,—and dost |thou| come unto me?
JND: I have need to be baptised of thee; and comest *thou* to me?
jpB2: I need you to baptise *me*,' he said. 'Surely *you* do not come to me?'
Simp: I need you to immerse **me**, yet **you** are coming to me?

JND is the most consistent in indicating such emphasis (by means of *italics*), while Simp is fairly consistent in the NT (by means of **bold** type). GNB occasionally uses italics for emphasis ('*all* things 1 Cor. 15:27), as do jbP and LBP 1 Jn. 2:25; 3:1, 9—unfortunately, the latter also uses italics for words supplied in translation! (1Jn. 1:10; 2:8) (See 13.5)

More modern versions may sometimes use special wording to indicate emphasis.

1 Sam. 15:12
REB: The Lord sent me to anoint you king
JND: Jehovah sent *me* to anoint thee king
NJB: I am the man whom Yahweh sent to anoint

Isa. 49:25
TEB: I will fight your enemies. I will save . . .
NJB: I myself shall fight those . . . and I myself . . .

Jer. 51:62
KJ2: O Jehovah, You have spoken against this . . .
NRS: O Lord, you yourself threatened to . . .
NJB: You, Yahweh, have promised to destroy . . .

2 Pet. 1:18
CEV: We were there with Jesus on the holy m.

NJB: We ourselves heard this voice from . . .
JND: and this voice *we* heard uttered from . . .
Simp: **We** heard this Voice come from heaven!

2 Sam. 24:17
KJ2: Behold, I have sinned. Yea, I have acted . . .
NRS: I alone have sinned, and I alone have done
NJB: I was the one who sinned. I was the one . . .
REB: It is I who have sinned, I who committed
GNB: I am the guilty one. I am the one who did . . .

Jer. 1:17
KJ2: And you must gird up your loins, and rise
NJB: As for you, prepare yourself for action.
TEB: Jeremiah, get ready. Stand up and speak . . .

Tit. 3:5
CEV: of any good things / that we have done.
NJB: . . . upright actions we had done ourselves;
JND: . . . in righteousness which *we* had done,
Simp: . . . any good deeds that **we** ourselves did.

1 Tim. 6:11
NJB: But, as someone dedicated to God, avoid . . .
CEV: Timothy, you belong to God, so keep away
JND: But *thou*, O man of God, flee these things,

Older versions usually ignore the above kinds of emphasis, while modern versions are far from consistent in their attempts to indicate emphasis; therefore, no evaluation of versions is made on this basis, except in favour of JND and Simp.

In Hebrew, there is a grammatical construction which emphasizes the verb. This is sometimes translated awkwardly, especially in older versions, and sometimes ignored.

Jer. 7:5
REB: If you amend your ways . . ., deal fairly . . .
NJB: if you really amend . . . if you really treat . . .
KJ2: if you thoroughly amend . . . truly practice

Gen. 22:17
KJV: in blessing I will bless thee
NRS: I will indeed bless you
REB: I shall bless you abundantly

In Greek, the so-called 'historic present' tense, used for vividness in narrative, for example, in Jn. 20, is usually ignored in modern versions (NAS uses * with the English past tense) while KJV used it quite freely, as well as RV, JND, YOU.

13.3 ARE OTHER WORDS MADE PROMINENT?

In the sentences of every language, all the words are not equal in prominence or emphasis; that is, some words are more prominent and some less prominent. At the beginning of a sentence, we expect to find the Topic of that sentence, while at the end we expect to find the Focus. (But extra emphasis can shift the latter to the beginning of the sentence!)

The most word-for-word translations are likely to reproduce the original beginnings and endings of sentences, and so reproduce the original Topics and Focuses.

But meaning-for-meaning translations can also use special wordings for the same purpose.

In Heb. 1:1, one can see how the original Topic (below left) and the original Focus (below right) have been changed in the upper sets of quotations, but preserved in the lower sets:

Heb. 1:1
Cass: God having spoken, in times of old, to . . .
REB: When in times past God spoke to . . .
Ster: In days gone by, God spoke in many and . . .
NRS: Long ago God spoke to our ancestors in . . .
TEB: In the past God spoke to our ancestors . . .

BLE: Fragmentarily and variously did God of old
Conc: By many portions and many modes of old,
NJB: At many moments in

Heb. 1:1
CEV: prophets spoke his message to our ancestors
Cass: an occasion and in many different ways—
NIV: prophets at many times & in various ways,
Simp: ancestors many times and in many ways;
Tran: the prophets in many and various ways.

Ster: ways to the Fathers through the prophets.
REB: . . . and varied ways through the prophets.
NRS: in many and various

the past and by many
KJ2: In many times and
many ways of old,
MOF: Many were the forms
and fashions in wh.

ways by the prophets
KJ2: God spoke to the
fathers in the prophets;
MOF: spoke of old to our
fathers by the prophets

1 Ki. 11:37
NRS: I will take you, and you shall reign . . .
REB: I shall appoint you to rule over all . . .
NJB: *You nonetheless I shall appoint to rule* . . .

Lk. 1:2
NAB2: just as *those* who were eyewitnesses from the beginning and ministers of the word *have handed them down* to
us,
NAB1 (NRS, NJB): as those *events were transmitted* to us
by the . . . eyewitnesses

Matt. 10:5
Ledy: Jesus sent out *these twelve* missionaries
NKJ: *These twelve* Jesus sent out and commanded them,

Jer. 4:30
REB (NRS): and seek *your life.*
NJB: *your life* is what they are seeking.

Matt. 26:11
REB: You have the poor among you always, but you will
not always have me.
Weym: *The poor* you always have with you, but *me* you
have not always.

1 Thess. 1:8
NRS: the word . . . has sounded forth *from you* . . .
REB: *From you* the word of the Lord rang out;

1 Tim. 3:16
CEV: Christ came as a human. / The Spirit proved / that he
pleased God, / and he was seen by angels. Christ was
preached / to the nations. / People in this world / put their
faith in him, / and he was taken up to glory.
NRS: *He* was revealed in flesh, / vindicated in spirit, / seen
by angels, / proclaimed among Gentiles, / believed in
throughout the world, / taken up in glory.

(Notice how the original Topic, preserved in NRS, is destroyed
in CEV.)

Jer. 33:18
GNB: there will *always* be priests ... to serve me and to offer burnt-offerings, ...
KNO: **never a lack of priest ... to wait upon me, bring me burnt-sacrifice ..., *day after day*.**

Certain particles like 'only' place emphasis on specific words and may be needed in translation for clarity of emphasis:

Lk. 12:41
NRS: are you telling this parable for us or for everyone?
REB: do you intend this parable **specially** for us or is it for everyone?

Jn. 4:2
REB: —although it was not Jesus himself but his disciples who baptized—
GNB: Jesus himself did not baptize anyone; **only** his disciples did [Deer]

Rotherham, both in his Emphasized NT of 1872/1913, and in his Bible of 1903, paid the greatest attention to questions of emphasis, with triple underlining for 'decided emphasis', and double underlining for 'slight emphasis', and several other marks for similar matters. But one wonders about the validity and reliability of his marking for emphasis, when such linguistic matters were not even discussed till about 100 years after Rotherham started his work.

Bible Society's Third Jubilee Bible (ed. Stirling) offers a graphic example of the varying significance of different parts of the Bible. The New Testament and much of the Old Testament is printed in two columns per page of normal type size; while various genealogies, itineraries, building specifications, detailed regulations, and tribal records (eg. Lev., parts of Jos. and Ki. and Chr.) are printed in three columns per page of smaller type. The latter are therefore presented as background material for the modern reader. (cf. also CCB)

13.4   QUESTIONS FOR EMPHASIS

Rhetorical questions, which are more frequent in the Greek New Testament than would be normal in English, are not real questions expecting answers, but rather emphatic statements. To prevent misunderstanding, they may be translated as affirmations or exclamations, or otherwise:

Matt. 5:47
NIV (cf CEV, NRS): Do not even pagans do that?
REB: Even the heathen do as much.

Jn. 18:35
KJV, REB: Am I a Jew?
NRS: I am not a Jew, am I? CEV: You know I'm not a Jew!

2 Ki. 13:8
NRS: . . . are they not written in the Book of the Annals of the Kings of Israel?
REB: . . . are recorded in the annals of the kings of Israel.

Matt. 26:55
NRS: Have you come out with swords . . .?
CEV: Why do you come . . .? REB: do you take me for a bandit that you have come out with swords . . .?

Rom. 8:31
KJV (cf NRS, REB): who can be against us?
CEV: can anyone be against us?

Jn. 16:31
KJV: Do ye now believe?
NIV: You believe at last!

Ps. 77:13
NAS: What god is great like our God?
TEB: No god is as great as our God.

Questions biased for a negative answer should normally take the English forms on the left below, while those biased for a positive answer should take the forms on the right:

Jn. 6:67 REB (cf NRS): Do you also want to leave?	*Jn. 6:42* NRS: Is not this Jesus, the son of Joseph, . . . ?

CEV: (asked) if they were going to leave him.
NAS (cf NIV): **You do not want to go away also, do you?**

Jn. 7:41
NJB: Would the Christ come from Galilee?
CEV: Can the Messiah come from Galilee?
REB: **Surely the Messiah is not to come from Galilee?**

Jn. 7:52
NJB: Are you a Galilean too?
CEV: **Nicodemus, you must be from Galilee!**

CEV: **Isn't he Jesus, the son of Joseph?**
GNB: **This man is Jesus . . ., isn't he?**
REB: **Surely this is Jesus, Joseph's son!**

Jn. 7:41
NJB, REB: **Does not scripture say . . .?**
CEV: **Doesn't this mean . . .?**

Jn. 7:25
CEV: **Isn't this the man they want to kill?**
REB: **Is this not the man they want to . . .?**

13.5   MISLEADING CASES

In this final section of the chapter, we briefly take up various typographical and other devices which seem to the uninitiated reader to indicate emphasis, but actually do not! In other words, many ordinary people are being misled by some of the devices we are about to touch on.

In 9.4, 12.5 and elsewhere, we have referred to simplified translations as consisting only of very short sentences, usually without any conjunctions. These give the misleading impression of a rather heavy information load, every short sentence being as important as its neighbour. [L Hohulin; Lewis, pp.179–80, 334]

Although in modern printed English (as in this book), italics is used to indicate light emphasis or the quotation of a foreign word, there has been a tradition in some printed English Bibles (KJV, RV, YOU, AMP, NAS, KJ2, RAV) of using italics to indicate where an English word or two has been supplied in translation to make up the sense, instead of [. . .] which might be more appropriate for that purpose (eg. NWT, JND):

Jn. 8:6 KJV: . . . and with *his* finger wrote on the ground, *as though he heard them not.*

Some Bibles print Old Testament quotations in the New Testament (14.7) either in italics (eg. NJB), or in capitals (eg. NAS), or in bold (eg. Stern, Cass). Any of these methods gives a misleading impression of emphasis, especially when the OT quotation consists of only a word of two.

RAV regrettably uses italics *both* for supplied words *and* for OT quotations!

Another misleading impression of emphasis is given in those versions which translate the divine name in the OT, not by 'Jehovah', but rather by 'LORD' or 'GOD' in all capital letters. The same applies to the NWT translation of 'you plural' as 'YOU' in capitals.

As in modern German, capital initials were used on every noun in the eighteenth-nineteenth centuries (see PUR, Will). Nowadays, they are restricted to the beginning of sentences and to proper names (Jesus) and titles (God, Holy Spirit, Son of Man).

But translators should ensure that they are not relying on capital initials on words like 'spirit, Spirit' or 'Son, son' in order to be understood correctly, since capital initials are obviously inaudible to a listener.

Capitalization has a way of extending itself to other terms which are themselves neither proper names nor titles, but are somehow related to them; in Heb. 1:1, we find 'Prophets' (GEN), 'Fathers' (GEN, KJV), and 'Truth' (AMP). Earlier editions of AMP tended to capitalize any terms which are even slightly related to the Divine. [Ellington, Pronouns]

It is also not satisfactory to, as it were, 'convert OT psalms to Christianity' by simply capitalizing various crucial terms (eg. Ps. 2 NIV: 'Anointed One, King, Son'), as this tends to prevent the psalm's interpretation in its original context. [Bratcher, NIV]

Some versions have extended capitalization to most or all pronouns referring to Deity.

No such practice was found in the original Hebrew or Greek, nor in versions in Latin or in French, Spanish, or German. It was not used in KJV nor in the 1602 Prayer Book.

The practice may have first been introduced into the classical Dutch version of 1637. But, in English, it did not catch on till the mid to late nineteenth century, first in hymnbooks, and in Young's Literal Version, presumably as an expression of Victorian piety. The practice seemed to have reached its peak in the 1930s to 1950s, since when it has gone down again except in some hymnbooks. [Sangster; Ellington, Pronouns]

The capitalization may be restricted to the personal pronouns referring to Deity ('He, Thee, Me') as in NBV, NAS, BEC, KJ2, NKJ; or it may be extended to the relative pronoun ('Whom, Whose') as in FEN, AMP.

> Wuest curiously does not capitalize these pronouns in Jesus' prayers to God (eg Lk. 9:11). Young uses 'He' for God and 'he' for Jesus, thereby neatly solving the potential ambiguity in Heb. 1:1–3, admittedly at a theological price. NKJ makes a mistake in Mk. 1:36 'Simon and those who were with Him' (Simon!) 'searched for Him' (Jesus). Such versions can get entangled in problems of application, for example when Jesus is referred to by his disciples or by his opponents: in Matt. 2:8 Herod is speaking of the 'C/child', and in Jn. 10:33 the Jews are speaking of stoning 'Y/you', so that AMP capitalizes, while Wuest does not! OT psalms and prophecies can be given immediate Messianic interpretations, simply by capitalizing a few pronouns (eg. Gen. 3:15 AMP; Isa. 53 NAS; Ps. 2 NBV).

However, only about 25% of whole-Bible versions indulge in this gratuitous practice, which not only adds to God's word, but also creates problems of application. In this respect, the majority of versions, from KJV to RV to RSV to LBP to NIV to RAV, have decided not to capitalize such pronouns.

14

Is it rightly divided?

'Rightly dividing the word of truth' (2 Tim 2.15 RAV, KJV, KJ2) is a familiar biblical expression, which I am using to introduce the investigation of some important features of Bible translations, which are not often discussed. Most of the dividing of a Bible version arises naturally out of the translators' understanding of the full meaning of the biblical message: what belongs together and where boundaries of different kinds can be drawn.

14.1 TESTAMENTS

The Old Testament was originally written in Hebrew and Aramaic; while, after a few centuries, the New Testament was originally written in Greek. So there can be no valid objection to the two Testaments being printed and published separately, nor to a clear distinction being drawn between them when published together as a Bible.

The Deuterocanonical books, also called the Apocrypha, which relate to the OT and inter-testamental periods, have usually been translated along with the two Testaments, from KJV and earlier, to REB and CEV. Although Roman Catholic versions (NJB, NAB, KNO) contain these books at various points throughout the Old Testament, it would certainly be preferable if they were grouped together like an extra testament, and so could be omitted in publication for Protestants (as with NRS, REB, CEV, GNB).

14.2 GROUPING OF BIBLE BOOKS

The original Hebrew grouping of OT books was the Law, or the five books of Moses; the Prophets, including not only Joshua, Judges, Samuel, and Kings, but also Isaiah, Jeremiah, Ezekiel, and the 'book of the twelve' minor prophets; and the Writings, containing all the other books not mentioned above.

Unfortunately, English versions of the Bible follow the ancient Greek Septuagint version's partly-chronological grouping by subject-matter. However, the artificial breaks in the middle of Samuel, Kings, Chronicles, and Ezra–Nehemiah could well be abolished, or at least minimized, as in BLE, REB.

It would not be unfaithful to the original Greek NT to group together Luke–Acts, as well as John–1–3 John–Revelation, each on the basis of common authorship.

But in fact only John's, Paul's, and Peter's letters are normally grouped together on that basis, with sub-groupings according to recipient (eg. 1–2 Cor., 1–2 Tim.).

As all the individual books of the Old and the New Testaments originally existed separately from each other, there can hardly be any objection to their separate publication, either individually, or in groups (eg. the books of Moses; the letters of Paul). These are known as 'portions' in Bible Society terminology; but they had already been produced in 1539 by Taverner. They are still needed in all parts of the world for the many who are unable or are unwilling to read any large book. [Meurer; Omanson, Oxford]

However, the best case is when the Bible is produced as one whole volume.

14.3 DIVISIONS AND SECTIONS

If a Bible book is relatively long, the translator should grasp the overall meaning well enough to indicate the *major divisions* in the translated text itself (as in GOS, REB, Weym), preferably with a clear numbering of the divisions (as in NAB, NJB). It is much less useful if the divisions appear only in the book's introduction (as in GNB, CEV).

Whether a Bible book is long or short, the translator can additionally indicate the *minor sections* of the book, preferably with a heading (as in GNB, NIV, RAV, TEB, BEC, Weym, Ledy), or possibly with the capitalization of the first few words (as in REB), or even with an asterisk (as in JND). [Blight]

The English versions which come out best in having both major divisions and minor sections clearly marked are NJB, NAB, Conf, Weym.

It is quite wrong to divide a version principally into conspicuous chapters. This is because many chapter breaks do not correspond with breaks in meaning; and because they are not original to the Bible, but were invented in the thirteenth century. Those versions which make chapter boundaries much too conspicuous include GRT, DOU, KJV, BBE, KNO, AMP, BLE, NAS, KJ2, cbWi. (Chapter *numbers* are of course needed for easy accessibility (15.5).)

14.4   PARAGRAPHS

The vast majority of English versions of the Bible are divided into normal sense paragraphs in prose, as well as into stanzas in poetry. The paragraphs may be longer, as in most cases; or shorter, in the case of those which assign different paragraphs to different speakers in dialogue (as in CEV, TEB, ETR, GNB, NIV, LBP, GOS, jbPh). Such shorter paragraphs are also easier to understand.

What is supposed to be paragraphing, either by means of a bold verse number (as in NAS), or by means of ¶ (as in KJV up to Acts 21 only), is so obscure as to be unnoticed by most readers.

14.5   'VERSES'

The fifteenth–sixteenth-century introduction of 'verse' numbering (to facilitate access) happens, regrettably, also to have produced the most devastating example of wrongly dividing the word of God, since GEN began the practice of *paragraphing according to these 'verses'*, thereby destroying the unity of the meaning in real paragraphs, and enabling readers to take 'verses' as proof-texts out of their context with impunity. The practice has continued in BIS, KJV, PUR, CHA, BBE, LAM, AMP, NAS, RAV.

14.6 DIRECT SPEECH

Where the words of speakers are actually quoted as direct speech, it is the normal modern practice to introduce and conclude such direct speech with double (") or single (') quotation marks. All versions follow this practice (except KJ2, AMP, LAM, KNO, BBE, JND, RV, KJV; Latt, Wues, ckWi).

NBV fails to mark direct speech where God is the speaker in the OT. FEN dramatizes his translation of Romans, etc. by introducing dialogue. The speakers in dialogue in Job and Song of Solomon are often identified (as in REB, GNB).

It is an unnecessary refinement to print Jesus' words in red (NKJ) or in italics (Spen).

14.7 OLD TESTAMENT QUOTATIONS

Quite a desirable refinement, however, is the printing of Old Testament quotations and allusions in the New Testament with some special typeface, preferably italic as in NJB, CCB, RAV, MOF, jbPh; or bold as in Stern, Cass, Week; or small capitals as in NAS, FEN, Weym; or spaced as in ABU.

14.8 POETICAL LINES

Within prose sentences, KJV and other versions intended for public reading are heavily punctuated with commas so that even an inexperienced reader can group words together sensibly.

The same effect is achieved by the short sense-lines used by Rotherham and F S Ballentine throughout their versions, and by NJB, NAB, MOF and Barc in some of the Gospels and Letters.

By far the most important exemplification of sense-lines is to be found in those versions which print poetry as such (see 10.3 for the versions which do so).

But almost all of these attempts are vitiated by the double-column format, which forces many, even up to half, of the poetical lines to run over into gratuitous extra-indented part-lines.

In Ps. 18, NRS has 198 lines, of which 39 run over by a single word; while GNB has 206 lines, of which 48 run over by a single word [Newman, Poetry, 406–7]:

NRS:
Ps. 18:4–5
The cords of death encompassed
    me;
    the torrents of perdition assailed
        me;
the cords of Sheol entangled me;
    the snares of death confronted
        me.

Ps. 18:19a, 25a, 28b
He brought me out into a broad
    place;
With the loyal you show yourself
    loyal;
    the Lord, my God, lights up
        my darkness.

GNB
Ps. 18:4–5
The danger of death was all round me;
    the wave of destruction rolled over
        me.
The danger of death was round me,
    and the grave set its trap for me.

Ps. 18:19b, 25a–b
    he saved me because he was pleased
        with me.
O Lord, you are faithful to those who
    are faithful to you;
    completely good to those who are
        perfect.

NJB:
Ps. 18:4, 19a, 25a, 28b
With Death's breakers closing in on me,
Belial's torrents ready to swallow me,
    he freed me, set me at large,
You are faithful to the faithful,
    my God lights up my darkness;

Ps. 19:14
May the words of my mouth always find favour,
    and the whispering of my heart,
in your presence, Yahweh,
    my rock, my redeemer.

So, the only versions to avoid such run-over lines are NJB, JB, NEB (not REB), BLE (which are each printed in single columns), as well as CEV.

In any case, most books, with the exception of reference books (like dictionaries and telephone directories) are printed in single columns, as in those above and KNO; and many NTs: Twen, Robe, cbWi, jbPh, Norl, ckWi, Conc, Wues, Beck, Barc, Cres, Tran, Simp, Cass.

15

How accessible is it?

Some Bible versions seem so forbidding in format that the potential reader feels reluctant to enter—access seems to be limited! But various devices have been used in versions so as to facilitate access to them.

15.1   DIVISION AND SECTION HEADINGS

In 14.3, we mentioned the dividing of the Bible text into larger divisions and smaller sections in some visible way. Now we are concerned with their actual headings or titles, which should identify, describe or preview the content that follows, and so help the reader to know what to expect in that division (as in NJB, NAB, REB, Weym) and in that section (as in NJB, NAB, TEB, NIV, GNB, CEV, RAV, Weym, etc).

Since these headings are not part of the Biblical text, they could well be centred (as in GNB) and printed in italics (as in REB), rather than in the more prominent bold. Weym and Twen have the section headings blocked into the text on the left. [Fry, Headings; Blight; Loewen, Headings]

Since chapter divisions are largely arbitrary and date only from the thirteenth century, chapter summaries (as in the original KJV, DOU, RAE, cbWi, etc) at the head of each chapter are not appropriate.

Since pages are even more arbitrary than chapters, varying from one edition to another, page headings are even less desirable (as in KJV, YOU, KNO, RSV, NWT, NBV, LBP,

NRS), unless they are actual repetitions of the current division or section headings (as in REB, NAB2).

15.2   BOOK INTRODUCTIONS

Most Bible versions have no introductions to the books of the Bible (eg. REB, NRS, TEB, RAV, KJ2). Although serious Bible students have access to background information elsewhere, most ordinary readers of the Bible, including regular churchgoers, never get to know anything about the books of the Bible except what is actually written in them. So a few Bible versions (GNB, CEV, Barc, jbP2) provide at least a basic and uncontroversial introduction to each book, dealing with matters such as authorship, original recipients, date, and the circumstances leading to its writing, slight historical and cultural background, the main themes, differences from similar books, and an outline of the book's structure. [Zogbo]

Regrettably, the book outlines in GNB and CEV are not reproduced in the texts of the respective books.

Much more substantial (and controversial) introductions are provided in NJB and NAB, and of course in study editions of other versions.

15.3   NOTES, GLOSSARY AND INDEX

Explanations of unknown or difficult concepts may be given in the translated text (especially in simplified versions, like Ledy), or more likely in notes, at the foot or in the margin of the page; but they are not acccessible enough either at the end of the volume (as in Tran, ckWi) or at the end of each book (as in BLE).

Generally speaking, information which is needed for only a page or two (eg. the meaning of a proper name; a manuscript or a translation variant) should be indicated in the text, either with the usual a, b, c, etc; or with * (Simp, ETR); or with n (TEB). [Smith, Footnotes]

Information which is needed repeatedly (eg. on historical, geographical, cultural, and theological terms) can hardly be repeated every time (as in ETR, Stern), but

should be indicated in the translation, either with *
(Tran) or d (TEB), referring to a glossary (or word list, or
dictionary, or topical concordance) at the end of the
volume (Tran; TEB).

Since there is no indication in the text, nobody knows
what 'difficult words' (CEV) are to be found in the Word
Lists or Glossaries of CEV, GNB, KJ2, NAB1, ckWi.

In contrast, you may have a Bible in front of you and
want to know what it has to say on a particular event,
topic, institution, person, or place. In a reference book,
you would turn to the index, but very few Bible versions
have any. Those that do are GNB with an index; NWT
with a general concordance; NJB with an alphabetical
table of the major footnotes; and NAB1 with a glossary
of biblical theology terms (with Bible references); TEB
with a topical concordance; jbP2 with a short index; Ledy
with a topical verse finder; and even TYN, GEN, BOO had
some such feature.

Since those who need the most help are likely to be
less than expert in handling large volumes, it would be
better to have only one alphabetical listing at the end (as
in TEB), rather than separating the Word List from the
Index (as in GNB).

15.4   CROSS-REFERENCES

These are references from one passage of the Bible to
another which contains the same or similar information,
eg. on proper names and important concepts. One can get
the same sort of references from a concordance. [Pritz]

Some versions (AMP, TEB, ETR) print OT references in
the NT in the translated text itself. Parallel passage
references, especially between the Gospels and between
Kings and Chronicles, are printed immediately beneath
the section headings in GNB, CEV; while all other references
are printed at the foot of the page (as in GNB, NAB) or in
the margin (as in NJB).

The first two types of reference are very important and

should certainly appear. But all cross-references could be put together, and be located in the margin just opposite where they are needed, to avoid the need for indicators in the text.

15.5   LOCATION OF VERSE NUMBERS

Verses were introduced only in the mid-fifteenth century for the OT and in the mid-sixteenth century for the NT, before which period chapters were simply divided into quarters with A, B, C, D. Ever since, verse numbers have become indispensable as a means of reference to the Bible text.

There are some discrepancies between the numbering of the Hebrew and the Greek originals of the OT; and (N)JB conveniently carries both numbering systems as alternatives.

A few versions (like jbP1) give only the first verse number for each paragraph, while a few (like Wues) give only the first and last verses. Peterson has no verse numbers.

Almost all Bible versions, however, give every verse its own number. Several of them (CEV, REB, NRS, TEB, ETR, KJ2, NAB, NIV, GNB, LBP, NBV, NWT, YOU) locate the number at the beginning of that verse, which can of course be at any point, left, right or centre, of the printed line, and so are tedious for the eye to search for.

But, in any case, verse numbers are not part of the Bible text and are never read aloud as such. Rather, they function as a means of reference to and from the text. They should therefore be readily visible to the eye as it skims down the page seeking a chapter-and-verse number. That requirement suggests that each verse number should be located in the lefthand margin of every page (as in BLE, ROT, Conc) or of every column (as in JND, RV). The same effect is incidentally achieved by those versions (RAV, NAS, AMP, LAM, BBE, KJV, GEN) which mistakenly paragraph by verses (14.5).

A few versions have the verse numbers in every right-hand margin (Twen, Weym). A few versions correctly keep the verse numbers in the margins, but locate them in left- and right-hand margins on alternate pages (NJB, NEB, KNO, GOS, MOF, BEC, jbP2), which is rather tiresome to the eye as it has to run in different directions on different pages to reach the beginning of the verse!

Those versions which locate the verse numbers in the margins can, where necessary, specify the actual verse beginning, either by inserting an extra space there (as in KNO), or by inserting a raised dot (as in NJB), or by a vertical bar (as in BEC), or even by repeating the verse number (as in Biblia Hebraica Stuttgartensia).

The best location for the contents of each page (eg. Jn. 2:12–3:13) is the bottom outside corners, as one realizes when using BLE, rather than the top outside corners or middle.

15.6   SEQUENCE OF BOOKS

Chapter divisions were introduced into the Bible in the thirteenth century, based on approximate equality of length within each book of the Bible. For ready access, the conventional numbering of chapters is usually followed, with the actual numbers boldly printed.

Exceptions are older Catholic versions made from the Latin Vulgate, which have slightly different numbering of most Psalms, and some other different chapter divisions elsewhere; and Swann and Schonfield, who each uses his own divisions and numbering.

Most versions follow the conventional sequence of books, which is almost always printed as the 'Contents' to versions (except YOU, BEC, ROT), which makes it convenient for those who already know that sequence.

Versions that do not follow the conventional sequence are JPSA, which follows the Hebrew sequence; FEN, Twen, and Scho, who follow an assumed chronological sequence;

and Swann, who has his own arrangement of sections throughout the NT; and CCB, whose OT is a blend of the Hebrew and the Greek sequences.

But those who do not know the conventional sequence should be assisted by an alphabetically-ordered 'Contents' in addition. It is best to have a single list covering the whole Bible, as in NRS, LBP, AMP, NWT; rather than two lists, one for each Testament, as in GNB, NAB1, KJV, since new readers may not know which Testament a book belongs to.

SUMMARY OF CHAPTERS 13–15

Chapters 5–9 dealt with matters of accurate translation of the original meaning; while chapters 10–12. dealt with the adequate expression of that meaning in the English language.

In chapters 13–15 we have been concerned with the presentation of the Bible translation—it could be in any language. We dealt first with the clarity of its pronoun references and the distribution of prominent items, both of which matters still fall within the province of the translator.

Then we moved on to matters which fall more and more within the province of the publisher: dividing the text into sections and paragraphs, and marking direct speech and OT quotations; and then providing easy access to the version in terms of introductions and section headings, glossary and index, the location of verse numbers and the sequence of books.

Were translators and publishers to follow all our recommendations, both serious and casual readers of the Bible would be helped to assimilate God's message to them more readily.

Assessing Bible Translations

16

Characteristics of an ideal translation

In chapters 2–15 we have fairly exhaustively gone through many characteristics which distinguish Bible translations from each other, ranging from the people who do the work and the underlying manuscripts; through accurate translation of the full original meaning, and use of natural, modern English; to clear, rightly-divided and accessible presentation.

Therefore, as a sort of summary embodying all the preferred characteristics that have been touched on, I now present a specimen of an ideal version for you to judge for yourself.

16.1 CHARACTERISTICS WHICH ARE NOT DIRECTLY VISIBLE

The translators should be an organized group (2.2), be international (2.3), be interdenominational (2.4), and be believers (2.5). They should know the original languages and cultures well (3) and use the best manuscripts of the original with as little emendation as possible (4).

16.2 VISIBLE IN THE VOLUME AS A WHOLE

Since a Bible is meant to be read frequently, it requires very strong binding (unlike my TEB and NIV!). Since it is also likely to be carried to church and elsewhere, it

should be as small and portable as possible (unlike my
GEN, NJB, NAB1, KJ2, BLE, TEB!).

At the very beginning, all the principles governing the
translation process, and its product in the form of the
version given, should be set out.

A single alphabetical list of the books of the Bible
(15.6) should precede the usual 'Contents' list of the
books in sequential order. Then, a list of any abbreviations
and symbols to be found in the version.

Each book of the Bible has a basic introduction to its
contents (15.2) along with an overall outline of its
structure, to be repeated within the text of the book.

In the Old Testament, the divine name appears as
Jehovah (7.2). Some psalms are translated as acrostics
(7.1).

At the end of the volume appears a single alphabetical
list combining glossary to explain recurring terms and
topical index to enable readers to find what they want.

16.3   VISIBLE ON THE PAGE

Even though both NAB1 and 2 look to me the worst of
all versions on the page, I wanted to show how a NAB1
page could be reformatted into a single column; and
eventually become a sample of an ideal page, as on the
following page.

So, the basic text is NAB1 of 1970, which is a meaningful
translation (8–9) in natural English including extra poetical format (10). It is modern (11.1), and approaches the
common level (12.3). Direct speech (14.6) is marked
normally with '. . .'.

However, shorter paragraphs (14.4) are introduced
from GNB. The text is made inclusive (11.2) at all
relevant points, according to GNB2. A manuscript variant
(4.), noted in GNB, is enclosed in [[. . .]] like NRS; while
some translational additions (8.5) from JND, KJ2 are enclosed in ‹ . . . ›. From JND and Simp, emphasis (13.2–3)
is indicated in bold. The fonts and location of the
division and the section headings (15.1) are modified.

Items indicated by *, drawn from TEB, ETR, Tran, are to be found (hypothetically) in the Glossary (15.3) at the end.

In the inner left margin are the verse numbers (15.5), with an extra space where necessary in the text to show the verse break. In the outer left margin are the chapter numbers, as well as numerous cross-references (15.4) drawn from NAB1, JND, NJB. In the right margin are notes (15.3) drawn from NAB1, JND, TEB, ETR, Simp. Notes are actually essential only for manuscript and translational variants, while most of those explaining terms and customs could rather be in the glossary.

At the bottom left of the page appears the page content reference (15.5) according to BLE.

11; 3:1, 20; 7:13; 9:22. 5:44; 10:42 11:45.	42	There were many, even among the Sanhedrin*, who believed in him; but they refused to admit ‹it› because of the Pharisees*, for fear they might be ejected	In 42 and also in 3:20, we see that there is no negation of freedom.
	43	from the synagogue*. They loved human approval rather than the approval of God.	43 literally, 'glory of people . . . of God.'

Summary Proclamation

11; 6:40; 13:20; 14:1 Matt. 10:40.	44	Jesus proclaimed aloud: 'Whoever puts faith in me believes not so much in **me** as in him who sent me;	44 him: God
14:7–9 1:1,9; 3:19; 8:12.	45	and whoever looks on **me** is seeing him who sent me.	
3:11, 17; Matt. 13:18–; Lk. 8:21; 11:28.	46	I have come to the world* ‹as› its light, to keep anyone who believes in **me** from remaining in the dark.	
8:37, 47; Deut. 31:26– 9; Heb. 4:12.	47	If people hear my words and do not keep ‹them›, *I am not the one to condemn them, for I did not come to condemn the world* but to save it.*	
	48	*Those who reject* **me** *and do not accept my words* already have their judge, namely, the word* I have spoken— it is that which will condemn them on the last day*.	

1:1; 3:11;
14:10, 31;
Deut. 18:18–
9; 6:63; 8:26–
8

49 For **I** have not spoken on my own;
no, ‹the› Father who sent me
has commanded me
what to say and how to speak.

49 *Father:*
God

50 Since I know that his commandment
means eternal life*,
whatever **I** say
is spoken just as he instructed me.'

III: THE BOOK OF GLORY

13.   *The Washing of the Feet*

2:4; 7:30;
8:20;
Matt. 26:17;
Acts 4:23.

1 Before the feast of Passover*, Jesus
realized that the hour* had come for him
to pass from this world to the Father. He
had loved his own in this world, and
would show his love for them to ‹the› end.

1 *Passover:*
one of the
most
important
Jewish
holidays. It
celebrated
deliverance
from Egypt.

6:71; 17:12
Matt. 26:20;
Lk. 22:3. 1:1;
3:35.

2 The devil* had already induced Judas,
‹son› of Simon Iscariot, to hand him over;
3 and so, during the supper,   ‹Jesus›—fully
aware that he had come from God and
was going to God, the Father who had
4 handed everything over to him— rose
from the meal and took off ‹his› cloak. He
picked up a towel and tied it around

2 *Induced:*
literally, 'The
devil put into
the heart that
Judas should
hand him
over.' It is
uncertain into
whose heart,
Judas' or
devil's?

Lk. 12:37;
17:7–10.

5 himself.   Then he poured water into a
basin and began to wash his disciples'
feet and dry them with the towel he had

5 *Basin:* the
exact vessel is
not certain,
but it was used
for washing,

Matt. 3:14.

6 around him.   Thus he came to Simon
Peter, **who** said to him, 'Lord*, are **you**
going to wash **my** feet?'

perhaps by
pouring, in
which case the
translation
should be
'pitcher'.

7 Jesus answered, '**You** may not realize
now what **I** am doing but later you will
understand.'

14:26. 2:19;
1 Cor. 6:11;
Eph. 5:26.

8 Peter replied, 'You shall **never** wash my
feet!'
'If I do not wash you,' Jesus answered,
'you will have no share in my heritage.'

10 *Bathed:*
many have
suggested that
this passage is
a symbolic
reference to

9 'Lord,' Simon Peter said to him, 'then
not only my feet, but my hands and head
as well.'

baptism. The
Greek root
involved is

15:3; 1:48.
6:70.

10 Jesus told him, 'Those who have bathed
have no need to wash [[except for their

used in
baptismal

1 Cor. 6:11;
Eph. 5:26;
Ti. 3:5;
Heb. 10:22.

11 feet]]; they are entirely cleansed*, just as **you** are; though not all. (The reason he said, 'Not all are washed clean,' was that he knew his betrayer.)

12 After he had washed their feet, he put his cloak back on and reclined at table* once more.

contexts. The washing of the feet was connected with Baptism in early Christian liturgy.

John 12:42–13:12

17

Weighting the assessment criteria

17.1 HOW OTHERS HAVE JUDGED THE CRITERIA

Kubo & Specht (1975) offered very sensible and clear 'Guidelines for selecting a version' (ch. 17) which cover three basic criteria: the underlying text of the original; accuracy in translation (the most important); and the quality of the English.

In Foster's book chapter 4 is on 'Viewing the standards' which seems to cover perhaps too many things: the most important, accuracy, in conveying the original form, meaningful message, spirit, naturalness, reader reaction, and text of the original; then, clarity of English for precise understanding; and then beauty of style, of sound, and of appearance on the page; with a caveat as to the dangers if the translators' beliefs do not accord with the scriptures, especially in relatively free (meaningful) translations, and in continuing ignorance of aspects of biblical times.

J L Jones also has his chapter 4 on 'How to choose a Bible', mentioning interest (readability) versus accuracy; the latter covers the underlying text of the original, as well as (ch. 5) translating either the words or the meaningful ideas.

Sheehan has eight principles (p.29–30), here slightly re-arranged: orthodox translators; a committee of translators; a cautiously eclectic text; language; the balance of words and meaning; the tendency to transculturalize; retention of technical terms; contextual translation.

On the subject of choosing Bible translations, all four of the above, the last two in small booklets, have written something well-balanced, sensible and applicable, with more or less the right conclusions, even though they are not fully conversant with translation principles.

In contrast, the following book by Van Bruggen is ill-informed, unbalanced, and confusing. He has seven 'Characteristics of a reliable translation' (ch. 5) (my numbering and my comments below):

1. faithfulness to the form, including both English style and the Hebrew/Greek words and sentences;
2. clarity, by which is meant the Reformation doctrine of Scripture as open to the people;
3. completeness, by which is meant the exclusion of the Apocrypha and of scripture as portions;
4. loyalty to the text, being the Masoretic OT and the Majority NT;
5. spirituality of the translators and of their translating 'blood, only-begotten', etc;
6. authoritativeness, covering 'Holy' in the title, physical format, and italics for supplied words;
7. ecclesiastical usage of technical terms.

1 puts together the two languages involved even though they are obviously apart; the meaning seems to matter less; 2 is in fact confused with accuracy of translation, while 'openness' is reduced by his 3,5, and 7; 5. overlaps with 7; 4. is misguided, and closely related in his thinking to 6, which is seen to be a very mixed bag, but is evidently his controlling principle. Following these guidelines would be very difficult and would lead to very unreliable conclusions.

17.2   THE CRITERIA ARE MULTIPLE

Did you choose a particular version of the Bible just because you inherited a copy from your grandparents, or because you won it as a prize at Sunday School? Or do you just follow the custom of your church or fellowship without even seeking the reasons for their choice? Or do you justify your choice of version by saying, 'I like it' or

'It's so readable'? None of these is a sufficient reason for sticking to a particular version of the Bible.

More seriously, is it legitimate to pick one single criterion on its own, and so settle the question? For example, 'All the translators hold to a high view of Scripture'; or 'All the translators are learned professors'; or 'They translate the New Testament from the Received/ Majority Text'; 'The translation is faithful to the form (words) of the original'; 'It is very meaningful'; 'The English is beautifully clear'; 'There are attractive illus-trations/scholarly footnotes'. Not one of these criteria, however important, can be sufficient on its own to lead anyone to prefer one translation over another.

Some translations will fare well on some criteria, but badly on others. What must be emphasized is that all the different criteria, mentioned from chapter 2 to chapter 15, ought to be taken into serious account before one can make an overall judgment on which versions are better than others.

On each criterion, I have graded the versions in relation to each other out of 10 as the basic score.

17.3   THE CRITERIA VARY IN IMPORTANCE

The criteria vary enormously in importance: some affect less than 1% of the whole Bible, while others affect close to 100% of the whole. Some affect only the written form, while others affect both the written and the spoken forms.

Therefore, I have ventured to multiply or divide each version's basic score out of 10 according to my estimation of the weight to be given to the different criteria.

We shall now go through all the criteria in turn, according to the sequence in chapters 2 to 15, noting the weighting factor, together with a few of the best and the worst examples in modern versions of the Bible or of the New Testament. For each section of the Table, the two-five criteria listed are given an approximate percentage of the total weighting. (Version abbreviations can be found in Tables 1–3 of ch. 1.)

Chapter	Criterion	Multiply by × divide by ÷	Some of the best:	Some of the worst:
2.2	translators in a group	÷ 3	most	LTB MKJ
.3	translators from different countries	÷ 5	NIV, GNB	LBP LTB
.4	translators from different denominations	÷ 3	REB, NRS	NAB NJB
.5	translators as believers	÷ 3	TEB, RAV	NWT MOF
		3%		
3.	up-to-date knowledge of biblical languages	÷ 3	REB, NRS	LTB BLE
4.	from best manuscripts with few emendations	× 1	GNB, NIV	RAV LTB
		4%		
7.1	some psalms as acrostics	÷ 10	KNO	all others
.2	God's name as Jehovah or Yahweh in OT	÷ 2	BLE, NJB	TEB LBP
8.	translating the full original meaning of words	× 10	GNB, TEB	NWT Conc
9.	and linkages within sentences	× 5	REB NJB	YOU Ledy
		44%		
10.1	expressed in natural English	× 3	REB CEV	LTB, AMP
.3	where appropriate, in poetical format	× 1	NJB, NAB	LTB LBP
11.1	in fully modern English	× 5	CEV, TEB	KJV KNO
.2	language inclusive of both sexes	÷ 3	NRS, CEV	RAV LTB
12.4	preferably, a common level of English	× 2	CEV, GNB	LTB AMP
		32%		
13.2	emphasis indicated with bold/italics	÷ 3	Simp/JND	most
.4	pronouns referring to God not capitalized	÷ 2	most	LTB, NKJ
		2%		

14.3	major division and minor section headings	÷ 2	NJB, NAB	NRS LTB
.4	normal paragraphing, preferably short	× 2	CEV, TEB	RAV NAS
.6	direct speech indicated with '. . .'	÷ 2	most	LTB, AMP
.7	OT quotations in NT in italics/capitals	÷ 5	NJB/NAS	LTB, BLE
		9%		
15.2	basic introductions to books of the Bible	÷ 4	GNB, CEV	most
.3	glossary combined with index	÷ 5	TEB (GNB)	most
.5	verse numbers located in left margins	× 1	BLE, JND	most
.6	alphabetical contents	÷ 6	NRS, LBP	most
		5%		

Approximately 44% of each score arises from chapters 5–9 on 'Accuracy of translation'; 32% from chapters 10–12 on 'English'; 16% from chs. 13–15 on 'Presentation'; and 7% from chapters 2–4 on 'Who Translates What?'.

After the basic scores out of 10 have been weighted as above, the total score for each version could total 351; but each score is then converted into a percentage for easier comprehension.

The basic scoring, together with the weighting, is intended to reduce somewhat the subjective element in my assessment of the overall quality of Bible translations.

That assessment, however, remains subjective. There-fore, if you disagree with my overall assessment of any version, it may be because you disagree with my weight-ing, or with my assessment of it on a particular criterion.

18

An Order of Merit

18.1 A RATING OF VERSIONS

Derived from the weighted scores outlined in chapter 17, we now present a rating, or ranking, or grading, of versions, according to the broad bands in the first column.

In the second column below, appear (in **bold**) the latest editions of Bibles, while plain type is used for earlier editions. In the third column, appear a few other, mostly older, Bibles whose scores have not been worked out in detail. In the fourth column, appear fairly recent New Testaments.

Band	Main Bibles	Other Bibles	New Testaments
9	**Good News Bible** (=TEV)		
8	**New Jerusalem Bible** **Revised English Bible** Jerusalem Bible	CEV	Translator's J B Phillips 1–2 Robertson (Weym) Stern
7	New English Bible **New International Version** New American Bible 1 **The Everyday B** (=ICB, NCV) **Goodspeed & Smith**		Barclay Beck Schonfield 1–2 Cassirer Simple English C B Williams Norlie C K Williams

Band	Main Bibles	Other Bibles	New Testaments
6	**New Revised Standard V** **New American Bible 2** **Moffatt** **Easy-To-Read V** (=EVf Deaf) **Living Bible Paraphrased** **Knox**		Wuest Cressman Confraternity Lattimore Ledyard
5	**New American Standard B** Revised Standard Version **New Berkeley V** (=MLB) **Revised Authorised Version** **Bible in Living English** **New King James Version**	Fenton Boothroyd	
4	**New World Translation** **Bible in Basic English** **Literal T of the B** (=KJ2) American Standard Version **Amplified Bible** **J N Darby** **Revised Version**	Lamsa Modern KJV ABU Sharpe C Thomson MacRae Rotherham Purver	
3	**King James Version** (= AV) **Challoner** (rev'n of Douay)	Geneva Tyndale Great Bible Coverdale Bishops	Concordant
2	**Young's Literal T**	Wyclif 2 Douay-Rheims	
1		Wyclif 1	

In the subsequent sections, we briefly go through the Bibles and the Testaments, noting their best (plus factor) and their worst (minus factor) characteristics. An excerpt of Heb. 1:1–3 is added where appropriate.

18.2 BIBLES

BAND **9**:

GNB 76:	Plus factors	Minus factors
translators familiar with linguistics and translation theory	Meaning-for-meaning; incl. linkages. Modern, natural English; sex-inclusive; common level. Poetical format. Best manuscripts, little emendation. Divisions & sections; direct speech. Translators in a group, international, inter-denominational. Book introductions; glossary & index; alphabetical contents.	(divisions shown in introduction, but not in text) (but not clear what is in glossary)

In the past, God spoke to our ancestors many times and in many ways through the prophets, 2. but in these last days he has spoken to us through his Son. He is the one through whom God created the universe, the one whom God has chosen to possess all things at the end. 3. He reflects the brightness of God's glory and is the exact likeness of God's own being, sustaining the universe with his powerful word. After achieving forgiveness for the sins of all human beings, he sat down in heaven at the right-hand side of God, the Supreme Power.

BAND 8:

NJB 85:	Plus factors	Minus factors
intended to replace JB of 1966, the first Catholic Bible from original languages to be completed.	Meaning-for-meaning; incl. linkages.	
	Modern, natural English; inclusive.	Literary level.
	One column format; poetry, also in NT.	
	From best manuscripts.	
	Verse numbers in alternate margins.	
	Yahweh.	
	Divisions & sections; direct speech;	
	OT quotations italicized.	
	Translators in a group, international.	All Roman Catholic.
	Book introductions; index.	
	One psalm acrostic.	

At many moments in the past and by many means, God spoke to our ancestors through the prophets; but in our time, the final days, he has spoken to us in the person of his Son, whom he appointed heir of all things and through whom he made the ages. He is the reflection of God's glory and bears the impress of God's own being, sustaining all things by his powerful command; and now that he has purged sins away, he has taken his seat at the right hand of the divine Majesty on high.

REB 89:	Plus factors	Minus factors
intended to replace NEB 1970 (one-column format)	Meaning-for-meaning; incl. linkages. Modern, natural English; inclusive. Poetical format. From best manuscripts. Headed divisions & unheaded sections; direct speech. Interdenominational translators.	Literary level. All from UK.

When in times past God spoke to our forefathers, he spoke in many and varied ways through the prophets. 2. But in this the final age he has spoken to us in his Son, whom he has appointed heir of all things; and through him he created the universe. 3. He is the radiance of God's glory, the stamp of God's very being, and he sustains the universe by his word of power. When he had brought about purification from sins, he took his seat at the right hand of God's Majesty on high,

BAND 7:

NIV 78:	*Plus factors*	*Minus factors*
	Fairly meaning-for-meaning; half-brackets for supplied words. Modern English. Poetical format. Best manuscripts, little emendation. Minor headed sections; direct speech. Translators in a group, international, inter-denominational, as believers.	Slightly word-for-word.

NAB 70:	*Plus factors*	*Minus factors*
intended to be replaced with the Revised NT 86, which is very word-for-word.	Meaning-for-meaning; incl. linkages. Modern, natural English. Poetical format, also in NT. From best manuscripts. Headed divisions & sections; direct speech. Translators in a group. Book introductions; glossary; alphabetical contents.	Slightly word-for-word also. But considerable rearrangements of 'displaced' verses. From USA, all Catholic.

TEB 88:	Plus factors	Minus factors
further simplified as: Easy-To-Read V. = English V. for the Deaf	Meaning-for-meaning. Modern English; common level. Poetical format. From best manuscripts. Minor sections; direct speech. Translators in a group, interdenominational, as believers. Glossary combined with index.	Lack of linkages, especially in ETR. Lord (not caps.) All from USA.

In the past God spoke to our ancestors through the prophets. He spoke to them many times and in many different ways. 2. And now in these last days God has spoken to us through his Son. God has chosen his Son to own all things. And he made the world through the Son. 3. The Son reflects the glory of God. He is an exact copy of God's nature. He holds everything together with his powerful word. The Son made people clean from their sins. Then he sat down at the right side of God, the Great One in heaven.

GOS 35:	Plus factors	Minus factors
Goodspeed, Smith, Meek, Waterman Gordon.	Meaning-for-meaning; incl. linkages. Excellent natural English. Best manuscripts; Poetical format. Verse numbers in outside margins. Headed divisions in OT. Translators in a small group.	but some emendations. From North America.

BAND **6:**

NRS 89:	Plus factors	Minus factors
intended to replace RSV of 1952	Modern English; sex-inclusive. From best manuscripts. Direct speech. Translators in a group, inter-denominational. Alphabetical contents.	Relatively word-for-word. From USA.

MOF 35:	Plus factors	Minus factors
Moffatt.	Meaning-for-meaning; incl. linkages. Natural English; poetical format. Best manuscripts; Verse numbers in outside margins. Direct speech; OT quotations italicized.	'The Eternal'. Literary level. but rearrangements and emendations; alleged Pentateuch sources shown. Translator one-man.

Many were the forms and fashions in which God spoke of old to our fathers by the prophets, but in these days at the end he has spoken to us by a Son—a Son whom he has appointed heir of the universe, as it was by him that he created the world. He, reflecting God's bright glory and stamped with God's own character, sustains the universe with his word of power; when he had secured our purification from sins, he sat down at the right hand of the Majesty on high;

LBP 71:	Plus factors	Minus factors
paraphrased from ASV of 1901	Meaningful; incl. linkages; Modern, natural English. Short paragraphs; direct speech. Translator a believer. Alphabetical contents.	but somewhat trans-culturized to USA. Colloquial level. No poetry. Lord (not caps.) Translator one-man, USA.

Knox 55:	Plus factors	Minus factors
first RC Bible since Douay-Challoner	Meaning-for-meaning; incl. linkages. Verse numbers in alternate margins. One-column format. Occasionally Jahvé Some psalms, etc. as acrostics.	Older English; literary level. No poetry. No direct speech. From Latin Vulgate. Latin name-forms. Lord (not caps.) Translator one-man, UK, RC.

BAND 5:

NASB 71:	Plus factors	Minus factors
updated ASV of 1901	Careful on tenses, etc. Poetical format. From best manuscripts. Verse numbers in left margins. Direct speech; OT quotes in capitals. Translators in a group, interdenominational, as believers.	Word-for-word. 'Verse' paragraphs. 'Divine' pronouns capitalized. From USA.

RSV 52:	Plus factors	Minus factors
from ASV; to be replaced by NRS of 1989	Poetical format. From best manuscripts. Direct speech. Proper names stressed. Translators in a group, inter-denominational.	Fairly word-for-word. From USA.

NBV 69:	Plus factors	Minus factors
revision of 1959	Poetical format. From best manuscripts. Direct speech, ... Translators in a group, interdenominational, as believers.	Fairly word-for-word. 'Divine' pronouns capitalized. except where God speaks. From USA.

NBV: God of old spoke to our Fathers at various times and in many ways by means of the prophets. 2. But He has at the end of these days spoken to us in His Son, whom He has appointed Heir of all things and through whom He made the world. 3. As the reflection of God's glory and the true expression of His being He sustains the universe by His almighty word. And when He had effected our cleansing from sin, He took His seat at the right hand of the Majesty on high.

RAV UK, NKJ US	Plus factors	Minus factors
1982:	Poetical format. Verse numbers in left margins. Headed sections; direct speech; OT quotations italicized. Translators in a group, international, inter-denominational, as believers.	Word-for-word. 'Verse' paragraphs. Not from best manuscripts. NKJ: 'Divine' pronouns capitalized.

BLE 72:	Plus factors	Minus factors
originally written in 1943 by Byington	Modern English. One-column format. Verse numbers in left margins. Jehovah. Direct speech.	Word-for-word. No poetry. No divisions/sections; no direct speech Translator one-man, USA.

BAND 4:

NWT 61:	Plus factors	Minus factors
revised 70	Supplied words in [ ]. Names stressed and syllabified. Modern English. From best manuscripts. Direct speech. Jehovah in OT; Translators in a group; Concordance; alphabetical contents.	Very word-for-word. Fairly unnatural English; little poetry but also in NT! Jehovah's Witnesses in USA.

NWT: God, who long ago spoke on many occasions and in many ways to our forefathers by means of the prophets, 2. has at the end of these days spoken to us by means of a Son, whom he appointed heir of all things, and through whom he made the systems of things. 3. He is the reflection of (his) glory and the exact representation of his very being, and he sustains all things by the word of his power; and after he had made a purification for our sins he sat down on the right hand of the Majesty in lofty places.

BBE 49:	Plus factors	Minus factors
In 'Basic' English, (which has very few verbs!).	Modern English; fairly common level; From best manuscripts. Verse numbers in left margins.	Fairly word-for-word. but awkward circumlocutions. 'Verse' paragraphs; no poetry. Lord (not caps.). No divisions/sections; no direct speech
	Translators in a group,	From UK.

LTB 87 =KJ2 82:	Plus factors	Minus factors
many editions, all by J P Green Sr.	Modern English. Jehovah. Glossary.	Very word-for-word. Unnatural English. No poetry. Not from best manuscripts. 'Divine' pronouns capitalized. No divisions/sections; no direct speech
	Translator believer.	Translator one-man, USA

KJ2: 1. In many times and in many ways of old, God spoke to the fathers in the prophets; 2. in these last days He spoke to us in the Son, whom He appointed heir of all; through whom He indeed made the ages; 3 who being the shining splendor of His glory, and the express image of His essence, and upholding all things by the word of His power, having made purification of our sins through Himself, He sat down on the right of the Majesty on high,

AMP 65:	Plus factors	Minus factors
	Some supplied words in [ ].	Several words for one original word. Unnatural, overloaded English.
	Verse numbers in left margins. OT quotations identified. Alphabetical contents.	'Verse' paragraphs; no poetry. Not from best mss. Lord (not caps.) 'Divine' pronouns capitalized. No divisions/sections; no direct speech
	Translators in a group, inter-denominational, as believers.	From USA.

JND 1890:	Plus factors	Minus factors
	Words supplied in [ ].	Very word-for-word. Old, unnatural English.
	Verse numbers in left margins. Jehovah. Emphasis indicated by italics.	No poetry. No divisions/sections; no direct speech
	Translator believer.	Translator one-man.

RV 1885:	Plus factors	Minus factors
slightly changed as ASV in 1901	Little poetical format. Verse numbers in left margins. ASV: Jehovah; . . . . Translators in a group, inter-denominational.	Very word-for-word. Old, unnatural English. RV: LORD. No divisions/sections; no direct speech. From UK/ USA.

BAND 3:

KJV=AV 1611	Plus factors	Minus factors
To many this has been *the* Bible!	'Classical' English, suitable for formal public occasions. Verse numbers in left margins. Alphabetical contents. Translators in a group, inter-denominational.	Word-for-word. Old English. 'Verse' paragraphs; no poetry. Not from best mss. From UK.

CHA 1772:	Plus factors	Minus factors
this is the commonly used revision of the 1610 Douay.	Verse numbers in left margins. Book introductions. Translators in a group, international.	Word-for-word. Old English. 'Verse' paragraphs; no poetry. From Latin Vulgate. Latin name forms. Lord (not caps.) No divisions/sections; no direct speech All Roman Catholic.

DOU: Diversely and many waies in times past God speaking to the fathers in the prophets: last of al in these daies hath spoken to vs in his Sonne, whom he hath appointed heire of al, by whom he made also the worldes. Who being the brightnesse of his glorie and figure of his substance, and carying all things by the word of his power, making purgation of sinnes, sitteth on the right hand of the Maiestie in the high places:

BAND 2:

YOU 1898:	Plus factors	Minus factors
started 1862	Poetical format. Jehovah. Direct speech.	Extremely word-for-word; but misunderstood Hebrew tenses. Old unnatural English. Not from best mss. 'Divine' pronouns capitalized. No divisions/sections. No contents. Translator one-man, UK.

1. IN many parts, and many ways, God of old having spoken to the fathers in the prophets, 2. in these last days did speak to us in a Son, whom He appointed heir of all things, through whom also He did make the ages; 3. who being the brightness of the glory, and the impress of His subsistence, bearing up also the all things by the saying of his might—through himself having made a cleansing of our sins, sat down at the right hand of the greatness in the highest,

18.3   NEW TESTAMENTS

Most of the New Testaments listed were basically produced by a single translator. Almost every translation is extremely meaningful. Most are in the preferred one-column format. A few other, less usual, both positive and negative, characteristics of the translations are given below, after excerpts from three of the best:

Tran: In the past God spoke to our forefathers by the prophets in many and various ways. 2. Now at the end of this age he has spoken to us by a Son. It was through him that God made the universe, and he has appointed him to enter into possession of the whole world. 3. He radiates God's glory, he shows us exactly what God's nature is, and by his powerful word he upholds the universe. When he had made it possible for man to be cleansed from sin, he sat down at the right hand of Almighty God in heaven,

CEV: Long ago in many ways and at many times God's prophets spoke his message to our ancestors. 2. But now at last God sent his Son to bring his message to us. God created the universe by his Son, and everything will someday belong to the Son. 3. God's Son has all the brightness of God's own glory and is like him in every way. By his own mighty word he holds the universe together.

After the Son had washed away our sins, he sat down at the right side of the glorious God in heaven.

Simple: Long ago, God used the prophets to speak to our ancestors many times and in many ways; 2. but, during these last times, God used *His* Son to speak to us. God appointed him to inherit everything. Through him God made the universe. 3. The Son is the shining brightness of God's glory and the exact picture of God's real being. The Son holds up the universe with his powerful word. After he had provided a cleansing from sin, he sat down at God's right side in heaven.

Band	NT	Date	Plus factors	Minus factors
8	Translator's (Bible Societies)	73	Meaning-for-meaning, incl linkages; common level; glossary. Group of translators, international	
	Contemporary Engl V	93	Meaning for meaning; common level. Introductions; sections; glossary.	But some loss or change of meaning.
	J B Phillips	58, 72	Short paragraphs. Index. 72: introductions.	58 freer than 72. 58: few verse numbers.
	Robertson (revised Weymouth)	29	Divisions & sections: vs nos in right margins; OT quotes in caps	Older, literary level. Divine pronouns capitalized.
	Stern	89	Index.	Full of Jewish terms.
7	Barclay	69	Some poetic format. Introductions	Slightly expanded meaning.
	Beck	63	Common level.	Divine pronouns capitalized
	Schonfield	56, 85	Introductions	Literary level.
	Cassirer	89	– – – – – – – – – – – – – –	Literary level.
	Simple English Bible	80	Common level. Bold for emphasis. Index.	Divine pronouns capitalized.
	C B Williams	37	Attention to tenses. Common level. Introductions. Very short paragraphs	Long headings to chapters. Divine pronouns capitalized
	Norlie	61	Common level	Divine pronouns capitalized.
	C K Williams	52	Fairly common level. Glossary.	No direct speech.
6	Wuest	61	Some supplied words in [ ].	Expanded level. No direct speech Divine pronouns

Band	NT Date	Plus factors	Minus factors
			capitalized. Few verse nos.
	Cressman 71	– – – – – – – – – – – – –	Simplified level.
	Confraternity	Divisions and sections.	Older English
	41	Group of translators.	All RC.
	Lattimore 82	– – – – – – – – – – – – –	Literary level. No direct speech.
	Ledyard 69	– – – – – – – – – – – – –	Simplified level. Divine pronouns capitalized.
3	Concordant Literal V 44	Verse numbers in left margins.	Absolutely word for word. Unnatural English. Divine pronouns capitalized.

We close with two further excerpts:

Latt: GOD, WHO IN ANCIENT TIME SPOKE to our fathers in many and various ways through the prophets, has now in these last days spoken to us through his son, whom he made the heir to all things and through whom he also created the ages. He is the gleam of his glory and the representation of his nature, he carries all things by his word of power; and when he had caused purification from sins, he took his seat on the right hand of the majesty, in the highest;

Conc: By many portions and many modes, of old, God, speaking to the fathers in the prophets, in the last of these days speaks to us in a Son, Whom He appoints enjoyer of the allotment of all, through Whom He also made the eons; Who, being the Effulgence of His glory and Emblem of His assumption, besides carrying on all by His powerful declaration, making a cleansing of sins, is seated at the right hand of the Majesty in the heights;

Coming to a Conclusion

19

Condemned?

Is it fair to condemn a Bible version out of hand, merely because one, or all, of the translators was/were Jehovah's Witnesses, or Catholics, or Unitarians, or 'liberals'?

Or because their NT Greek text was not the 'Received' or 'Majority' Text?

Or because they did not translate word for word?

Or because the level of English is too low—it reads like a newspaper?

Or because 'divine' pronouns are not capitalized?

Or because the version does not have 'Holy' in its title, or looks like any modern book?

Or indeed for the opposite of any of these reasons?!

The answer is that none of these considerations, taken singly, should prevent us from taking due account of the actual merits and demerits of any Bible version, multiple as they are. 'By their fruits you shall know them'. Otherwise, we would be jumping to unwarranted conclusions!

19.1 'IT IS NOT WORD FOR WORD!'

There are those, like J P Green, who would condemn out of hand all Bible versions which are not word-for-word translations.

211

'The Bible is not just another book, as our modern-day critics like to treat it. It is God-breathed, with depths that no man or men can fathom in this life. The Scriptures are so finely written as to meet the needs of totally diverse persons and situations. Only God can fit together *words* that will obtain the results which He has ordained from everlasting. Therefore, we contend that only a strict, *literal word-for-word* translation will retain all the depths and meanings which God has breathed into His *words*. To reword God's *words* is to rob someone or multitudes of the comfort, instruction, reproof, correction, etc. that they must have, and which God intends for them to have.' [CLW ?, p.3, my italics]

'The Word of God is sharper than a two-edged sword ONLY WHEN it is accurately translated, giving the true meaning of ALL *the words*. . . . The concept that the Bible should be predigested by Scholars, and spit out in another form, is straight *from Satan*. When the Bible is made to read smoothly like a newspaper, the *old Serpent is delighted*. For then those *words* which bring conviction of sin are NOT all there. Remember, the Spirit uses different *words* for various individuals in doing His work within them. If He did not think it necessary for each and every *word* that are in the Scriptures, He would not have breathed out the *words* modern translators count unnecessary. For a book claiming to be the Holy Bible to present itself to God's people without tens of thousands of the God-breathed *words* is absurd.' [S G T Perspective, 1993, p.1, his capitals and underlining, my italics]

This attitude stems from the constant mis-quotation of 2 Tim. 3:16 as if it said '*the words of* the Bible *are* 'God-breathed' (my italics for the additions to the quotation). It is actually 'all Scripture' that is said to be inspired or God-breathed; that is, every discourse, every paragraph, every sentence, every word, and every letter, together with their full meanings—it is not restricted to the words alone. No one would ever suggest rewording the original Hebrew or Greek; but if we are to translate at all, then rewording is inevitable simply because no two languages have the same words!

Such writers should rather 'stop *disputing about mere*

words; it does no good, and only ruins those who listen'
or read (2 Tim. 2:14 REB, my italics). They could be said
to be 'obsessed with disputes and *arguments over words,*
from which come envy, strife, reviling, evil suspicions,
useless wranglings, . . . (1 Tim. 6:4 RAV, my italics).

Such writers may also complain that the Bible's theological terms are not translated word-for-word. The translator 'is deliberately trying to eliminate from the TEV the
rich theological words which explain the doctrine of
salvation.' [Custer & Neal, p.16] For example, they prefer
'repentance' to 'turn away from your sins' [p.14] But
surely the latter (with more words) explains the doctrine
more meaningfully than the former (with the single
abstract word)?

19.2 'IT IS NOT FROM THE RECEIVED TEXT!'

Our chapter 4 gave the correct information on the original
manuscript situation; and therefore we downgraded
slightly those versions which did not make use of the
oldest and best manuscripts.

But a few writers, like J P Green, would condemn out
of hand all versions which do make use of them, and
have gone so far as to misinform the public as follows:

> 'In the first four centuries of our Lord, numerous *heretics*
> put forth *corrupted* versions of God's Word in order to
> maintain their God-dishonoring views, and to frustrate the
> true believers.' [CLW Oct89–Jan90, p.16, my italics]

> 'Here it is important to again consider the fact that in the
> second and third centuries after the Holy Scriptures had
> been completed, *heretics set about making changes* in order
> to establish their own man-centered theology. Among these
> were the Gnostics, ... [T]here are quite a few places in the
> NT where the NASB has foolishly adopted those formulations
> of the early heretics. And they have done this in the face of
> some very extensive witnesses from thousands of manu-
> scripts, and dozens of the early church fathers, that those
> readings are false, are not the original God-breathed words.'

> [These heretical changes] 'were of course opposed fiercely
> and steadfastly by the early believers. And the result is that

not many of those *corrupted* manuscripts have survived. A
few fragments have been dug up from the Egyptian sands
[in the twentieth century], but it was not until centuries
later [than it was written] that Codex B [Vaticanus] was
discovered, an almost complete m[anuscript] (believed to
have been executed about 325 AD). And it was not until the
early 1800s that Tischendorf picked another *corrupted*
m[anuscript] (the Sinaiticus, known as Aleph) out of a
waste-basket in a monastery. This one supposedly was
executed about 375 AD. It had been edited, and re-edited at
least ten times. Yet using these two *corrupt* m[anuscripts],
which disagreed over 3000 times with each other, ... the
unbelieving German critics joyously began to reconstruct
the Greek NT.' [CLW, Jul–Oct 1990, p.13, my italics]

The NIV translators 'used the "standard Hebrew text, the
Masoretic Text" ... But how did they use [it]? They admit
up front that they consulted the Dead Sea Scrolls, the
Samaritan Pentateuch "and the ancient scribal traditions
relating to textual changes." Ho! Look at the leeway they
give themselves again in order to change whatever they
judge needs to be changed. What ever happened to those
words that were "made certain" as the prophets were
"borne along by the Holy Spirit"? Did some of them get lost,
and were preserved for us only in the *sectarian, unbelieving*
scribes of the Dead Sea Scrolls, the Samaritan Pentateuch,
and in ancient scribal traditions? Yes, and in the Alexandrian
production, the Septuagint?' [CLW Oct 89–Jan 90, p 11–2,
my italics]

For any ancient book, whose original no longer exists,
scholars compare all existing manuscript copies (where
they disagree) in order to deduce what was originally
written. Normally, the older the manuscript, the better,
because it has fewer accidental changes, as well as fewer
deliberate changes, whether 'corruptions' by heretics or
'improvements and corrections' by the orthodox. But
those who hold the sentiments quoted above would base
their Old Testament on the ninth-century AD Masoretic
Text only; therefore, they have to abuse the much older
(BC) witnesses to the original OT as having been produced
by 'unbelieving sectarian' heretics!

Likewise, they would base their New Testament on the

seventeenth-century AD Received Text only, itself based on the many fifth-century and later manuscripts, with all their harmonizing 'improvements'; therefore, they have to abuse the fewer and older (first–fourth century) witnesses to the original NT (which came to light from the seventeenth to the twentieth centuries) as having been 'corrupted by heretics'! (The fact that these witnesses to the text sometimes disagree, incidentally, implies that they are independent of each other, and so can be validly used to deduce the true original.)

Those who thus advocate the MT and the RT as the manuscript base of all Bible versions (eg. KJV, NKJ, KJ2) go so far as to say:

> 'The Christian who rejects the King James Version and adopts one of its modern rivals by this very action places himself on the high road to *modernism*. For along with the KJV he has *rejected the only concept of the providential preservation* of Scripture which gives him any assurance that a pure New Testament text has been preserved down through the ages and is obtainable today. He has *rejected the view* that the special providence of God has operated in the sphere of the *Greek Church* and expressed itself in its usage and that therefore the *Byzantine text*, found in the vast majority of NT manuscripts (of which the Reformation (*sic!*) Text (Textus Receptus) is the historic printed edition, of which the KJV is the classic English translation), is a trustworthy representative of the divinely inspired original text and the *best of all extant texts*. And not only this but he has adopted *other concepts* of the providential preservation of Scripture, concepts which suggest that *God does not really care* whether or not a pure NT text is available to his people or whether or not his people have any assurance concerning the purity of the NT texts available to them.'
>
> ... Thus the rejection of the KJV for one of its modern rivals leads first to rejection of the doctrine of the providential preservation of Scripture, then to the the *rejection of the infallibility of Scripture*, and finally, to the *adoption of a modernistic religion* which rests not on the authority of Scripture but on *human reason*. [E F Hills The King James Version Defended, quoted in Paisley, p.89–90, my italics]

Since about 97% of the NT text is not in dispute, and

216 Coming to a conclusion

almost all of the rest can be readily established, to most
people this would clearly demonstrate God's providential
preservation of Scripture.

It is quite ironical that Hills, Paisley and others, consider
that it was *only* in the usage of the Greek Church (which
originated as the eastern half of the Catholic Church in
the break-up of the Roman Empire) that God preserved
the true NT text! It is ironical because those who hanker
after the 'good old KJV' (including its underlying text) as
their supreme authority seem to have their Christianity
rooted, *not* in the first-century NT Church and certainly
not in the later Catholic Church, but rather in the *seventeenth century* (the 'age of faith') which produced not
only KJV, but also the Received Text of the Greek NT
(significantly called the *'Reformation* Text' by Hills), and
'the Historic Creeds of the *Christian* Churches', viz. the
Westminster Confession of Faith and the Baptist Confession of Faith [Paisley, p.89–91, my italics].

This background helps us to understand the fanatical
intolerance shown by such people to all other versions,
and indeed to all other (non-'Reformed') denominations.

19.3   'IT IS FULL OF HERESIES!'

Some have to condemn out of hand any version made by
Jehovah's Witnesses, or by Catholics, or by . . ., because
they must be full of heresies. Whether or not such a
version actually contains any heresies, they would refuse
even to look at it!

It is true that there are some heretical doctrines to be
found in NWT (eg. the incoherent polytheism in Jn. 1:1
'The Word was with God, and the Word was a god'), but
the percentage of the whole Bible thus affected (I have
looked!) does not reach even 0.1% of the whole, which
is very far from 'full'.

If one takes the trouble to read any version at all, one
will find that none is produced for the prime purpose of
suppressing or perverting some Christian truth, as writers

of pamphlets and booklets often allege. It is true that a specific doctrine may not appear equally obviously in every expected verse in every translation; but the reason is usually manuscript variation, and sometimes translational variation. In any case, every Christian doctrine can be established from any Bible version, taken as a whole, as we demonstrate now.

Although 'The Spirit itself' (Rom. 8:16, 26 KJV) implies non-belief in the personality of the Holy Spirit, yet this inference is not supported by 'he', the Spirit of truth (Jn. 16:13 KJV).

Although NEB and REB have been accused of playing down the deity of Christ, this is actually clearer in 'our great God and Saviour Christ Jesus' (Tit. 2:13 REB) than in 'the great God and our Saviour Jesus Christ' (KJV); see also Rom. 1:4 GNB. Despite its Jn. 1:1, 18 and 8:58, NWT still has 'I and the Father are one' (Jn. 10:30) and 'My Lord and my God!' (Jn. 20:28).

Although in Isa. 7:14 GNB, REB, NRS, NJB all correctly have 'young woman' to translate the Hebrew word, in Matt. 1:23 all four translations again correctly have 'virgin' to translate the Greek, as well as other unmistakable indications of Mary's virginity.

Although 'through his blood' appears at Col. 1:14 in KJV, it is omitted from most modern versions (REB, NJB, NAB, NRS) simply because it is not supported by the Greek manuscript evidence; but the same phrase does appear in all versions at Eph. 1:7. GNB1 also has 'The blood of Jesus, his Son, purifies us from every sin.' (1 Jn. 1:7). 'They have washed their robes and made them white in the blood of the Lamb.' (Rev. 7:14)

To whoever says, with J P Green: 'Woe to those who put their trust in "Bibles" which have been shorn of such essential doctrines as . . .', it must be replied that there is in fact no Bible translation which has been so shorn!

19.4   'IT IS NOT EVEN A BIBLE!

Custer & Neal call their booklet against GNB/TEV: 'A Critical Analysis of a Dangerous Scriptural Perversion'. Which shows how ignorant they are of the issues involved.

Paisley's latest tirade against modern versions is called 'The Antichrist Bible', which turns out to be REB. He says:

> 'The *false* REB is *from hell*.' (p.83, my italics)
>
> 'In these ecumenical times the strategy is to *counterfeit* the Bible, and, of course, pass off the *counterfeit* as the genuine article. . . . You can see that demonstrated all around you by the multiplicity of *counterfeit Bibles* which are rolling off the printing presses today and flooding the country. Starting with the RV at the end of the [nineteenth] century, going on to the ASV, . . . going on to the NEB on which this new REB has its basis, the Good News for Modern Man, the LB[P], the NAS Bible and the NIV, the multiplicity of *counterfeits* continues to increase.' (p.87, my italics)
>
> 'Should the REB reach the lofty heights of eminence set for it by its sponsors that will most certainly be the crowning day for *German rationalism and unbelieving higher criticism*. Under the *guise* of scripture the REB is the great charter of *another gospel*.' (p.97, my italics)

But J P Green should probably get the prize for the sheer volume of his fanatical tirades against all versions, except KJV and his own LTB=KJ2!

> 'You will see in this volume [*Unholy Hands on the Bible II*] that the new versions are *adulterating* the precious Word of God. And they are spreading like a *plague* throughout the world! OVER 140 MILLION of the six volumes [NAS, NIV, NRS, NEB, GNB, NAB] we are reviewing are now out there *parading* as the Holy Bible. Yet each of them have *contra-dictions* within their covers, and collectively they contradict each other nearly 200 times. This *chaos and resultant confusion* is the result that *so-called* scholar-translators believe they can *do their own thing*, rewriting Scripture *to suit themselves*. Help us fight this attempt to *rob us* [of] the pure and unadulterated Word of God . . . ' [SGT Perspective, 1993, p.1, his capitals, my additions and italics]

'Christian people by the millions are being *duped into thinking that these smooth, gutted* new versions are really the God-breathed Scriptures.' (p.1, my italics)

'The modern versions have already *stolen away* over 1000 of 200,000 words of the NT, and have added instead far more *counterfeit words of their own.*'

'Today [the American Bible Society] is flooding the world with a *sad representation* of God's Word which they entitle 'Good News for Modern Man'—and that is truly *bad news* for anyone who puts any dependence on it.' [CLW, July–Oct 90, p.51, my italics]

Beyond the above attempts to put doubts into the minds of those who use these Bibles, he tries to instil fear into the ignorant by means of threats like these:

'BEWARE that you do not find yourselves charged as an *accessory after the crime* (2 Pet. 3:17) . . . If you come to know that men, however noted as reputable scholars they may be, are adding to the Word of God, and taking away the *words* of God, and *changing the plain and clear meaning of the words of God*, and you acquiesce in that breaking of God's commandment, then you will be *charged by God as an accessory.*' [CLW 1.2, 1989, p.1, his capitals, my italics]

'*YOUR CHILDREN AND GRANDCHILDREN MAY NEVER* SEE the Scriptures as you know them. . . . If *you allow the changes* now being made in the new versions, what will the next generation do to it? The *enemy is sowing seeds of unbelief* in the very Bibles you are handing your children to read.' (p.2, his capitals, my italics)

'Those who persist in using (NIV) and in calling it a Holy Bible, should be *warned that God will not be pleased.*' (CLW, 4.2, 1992, p.7, my italics)

From all this, one begins to wonder if he can still tell the difference between good news and bad news, between the genuine and the counterfeit! In fact, such an attitude is getting very close to the Pharisees' accusing Jesus of operating by means of the ruler of the demons.

The only way of understanding such an attitude is to assume that (despite all the harmonizing 'improvements' of its Greek NT text) KJV **is *the* Bible**, the product of the

Reformation, which is identical with the 'historic Christian faith'. (The Trinitarian Bible Society has as one of its aims: 'To uphold the doctrines of *reformed* Christianity' (my italics).)

Then, the older manuscripts (without these 'improvements', and even though only a tiny proportion of the total Bible is affected), which were subsequently discovered, have to be condemned as heretical. Likewise, the current policy of translating the full original meaning, rather than merely the words, which inevitably produces a fresh set of words in such translations.

Those who are opposed to these post-Reformation developments are then forced to mis-quote 2 Tim. 3:16 as if it said: 'All [the words of] Scripture [are] inspired by God . . .', so that their obsession with the KJV words can be legitimized!

Some also want to treat the Bible as a legal document, characterized by mini-paragraphs conspicuously numbered with chapter-and-verse for easy quotation, even out of context; and by its archaic language, so obscure to the lay person that a 'learned scribe' is needed to interpret it according to 'the tradition of the elders'. And KJV readily fits into this scenario too!

Against such attitudes we may quote Scripture—from any version!—as follows:

'They have zeal to God, but *not according to knowledge*.' (Rom. 10:2 KJ2, my italics)

Timothy was 'to instruct certain people to give up teaching *erroneous* doctrines . . . which . . . do *not further God's plan for us* . . . Through lack of [love . . . pure heart, a good conscience, and . . . faith] some people have *gone astray into a wilderness of words*. They set out to be teachers of the law, although they do *not understand* either the words they use or *the subjects about which they are so dogmatic*.' (1 Tim. 1:3–7 REB, my italics)

'And in fact there are many people . . ., who talk nonsense and *try to make others believe it*, . . . *They must be silenced*:

people of this kind *upset whole families,* by teaching things
they ought not to, . . .' (Tit. 1:10–1 NJB, my italics)

It seems that those who condemn all modern versions
as 'not even Bibles' are deceiving the (less-informed)
Christian public, by sowing seeds of doubt and unbelief
in their minds. Thus, like the Pharisees (Jn. 8:38–41),
they are actually serving the interests of the devil! So we
should pray that

'God may then grant them a *change of heart* and lead
them to *recognize the truth*; thus they may come to their
senses and *escape from the devil's snare* in which they have
been trapped and held at his will.' (2 Tim. 2:25–6 REB, my
italics)

Instead of these modern versions, they want people to
read literal, if not archaic versions (like LTB, KJV),
against which intention we can say (my italics):

'Blind guides, who strain out the gnat, but *swallow the
camel!'* (Matt. 23:24 KJ2)
'Why do you look at the speck of sawdust in your
brother's eye, with never a thought for the *plank in your
own?'* (Matt. 7:3 REB)
'Woe to you, lawyers! For you have *taken away the key
of knowledge.* You did not go in yourselves, and those who
were trying to go in, *you prevented.'* (Lk. 11:52 REB)
'In this way *you make God's word ineffective for the sake
of your tradition* which you have handed down.' (Mk. 7:13
NJB)

The paranoia of the above authors, however, is far sur-
passed by Riplinger in *New Age Bible Versions,* where
she claims that only KJV is God's translation, and that
ALL 'new' versions over the past one hundred years are
part of a satanic conspiracy to advance the One World
Religion of the New Age movement. Her claim is based
partly on a preference for KJV's Greek text; but mainly on
'the direct hand of God', she says. It also seems to involve
a phobia against the word 'new' and even the sound 's'
(as in satan, serpent). She actually plays a game, as

instructed by 'God', with the initials of some version names to prove they have 'sin'; and she seriously misquotes and deceitfully maligns various scholars responsible for some texts and versions. It should therefore be clear what is the real source of her inspiration. (Passantino)

20

Recommended!

20.1 WHICH BIBLE IS THE BEST FOR ME?

Contrary to the fanatical and uninformed sentiments quoted in ch. 19, there is no Bible version that is so bad overall that it should be condemned out of hand. 'The poorest is better than none.' 'The basic duties to man and God can be learned from *any translation* that men read prayerfully.' (Lewis, p. 365–6, 10–1, my italics)

A more Christian attitude than those quoted would be the following:

If we have cause to be suspicious of any Bible version, we should first of all 'carefully *examine the Scriptures daily* [in that version] as to whether these things [are] so' (Acts 17:11 NWT, my addition and substitution).

More than likely, we can then go on to say: 'in every way, whether in pretense or in truth, *Christ is being publicized*, and in this I rejoice' (Phil. 1:15 NWT (my italics))

The Wyclif 1380 translation was the first to break the bondage to ignorance of English-speaking Christians without any Bible to read; for that we must be very grateful. Others in the following two centuries risked their lives, and committed their time and energies, to improving English translations of the Bible; they did their best for their generations, and we are grateful to them too. Their versions are of immense historical and scholarly importance and interest to the English-speaking world.

But, from the table in 18.1, we saw that these Bible versions are rated in the lowest Bands (1–4), which means they are far from being the best from our present vantage point.

How can we, English speakers of the present day, who have access to several versions ranked in Bands 9 and 8, and 7 and 6, continue to hanker after those in the lower Bands?

In the highest Band in the rating, we find GNB, which conveys the full meaning of the original in modern English of a common level; so it is recommended for general use for everyone and should be generally available in Christian homes and in local churches, for members and visitors to use, and also to purchase from church bookstalls.

But it would be a serious mistake if any Christian or any congegation were to be confined to just a single Bible version at all times and for all purposes. [Fee & Stuart, ch. 2, esp. p.42; Lewis, p 10] This is because, however good that version is, it can hardly be perfect in conveying the original meaning accurately every time, even when there are manuscript disagreements or uncertainties as to what the original meaning is, or normal modern English is inadequate to express some stylistic subtlety of the original.

In the next two Bands of the rating, we find NJB, REB, NIV, TEB, NAB1, as well as JB, NEB, and GOS. Every home if possible, and certainly every local church, should also have copies of at least the first five of these, so that members and visitors can see and try out the versions for themselves, and then perhaps go out and buy one or more to use.

If possible, every church library should also have copies of the versions listed in the next two Bands: NRS, ETR, LBP, NAS, NBV, RAV/NKJ, as well as NAB2, MOF, KNO, RSV, BLE.

However, if we also take account of individual differences among readers, we may suggest that, in addition to GNB, the better-educated could use NJB and REB, as well as GOS and MOF; while the less-educated could use TEB and if necessary ETR, before trying GNB.

Those of certain Christian backgrounds might prefer either NIV and LBP, or NJB and NAB1 (which is better than NAB 2); while those who find it too hard to break with the KJV tradition might prefer NRS.

'Most available Bible translations are good. [But w]e may well find that some translations are *better for some purposes than others.*' (J L Jones, p 40, my italics)

If we further take account of different purposes to which the Bible version is to be put, then we suggest either GNB, or NIV, NAB1, or NJB, REB, for public reading, depending on the Christian and educational backgrounds of the congregation members.

For reaching out to the youth and outsiders, we suggest GNB or TEB or LBP, again depending on their background.

For general Bible study without any access to commentaries or reference-books, we may suggest the very fully-annotated NJB and NAB, or study editions of other versions; while for detailed word-studies and similar interests in the original languages, we suggest either a very literal version like NAS, NWT, LTB=KJ2; or preferably an interlinear version (Kingdom, Marshall).

From the above suggestions, you can see that, although GNB can be recommended for general use by everyone, I am also recommending other additional versions for different readers and for different purposes.

What aspects of God's message to mankind can we find in the versions of Bands 1–5 which we cannot find more accurately and clearly and in better English in the versions of Bands 6–9?

20.2   OUR RESPONSE TO GOD'S WORD

Only too often, even today, the Word of God, especially
in the versions in the lower Bands, seems to people more
like a blunt instrument which makes a heavy but unclear
impression upon them, rather than as something '*alive
and active* [which] cuts more keenly than any two-edged
sword, *piercing* so deeply that it divides soul and spirit,
joints and marrow; . . . *discriminat*[ing] among the purposes and thoughts of the heart.' (Heb. 4:12 REB, my
substitutions and italics)

As we have recommended, anyone who wishes to
receive God's Word can do so most readily by turning to
one or more of the Bible versions in the top Bands of our
Order of Merit (18.1).

'But a *natural* man does not accept the things of the
Spirit of God; for they are foolishness to him, and he
cannot understand them, because they are *spiritually*
appraised.' (1 Cor. 2:14 NAS, my italics) 'No matter how
a passage is worded, how closely or loosely translated,
the unsaved man will never understand it *unless the
Spirit of God opens his eyes* to its truth. In this respect,
the Word of God is most definitely given to His people.
Through it God gives instruction on how to live in a right
relationship with Him. It is His Word to us, and must be
treated, *not merely as a glorious piece of literature,* but
as *the very Word of God*. The most important aspect of
translation, therefore, is not the audience but the *Author*.'
(Andersons, p.6, my italics)

Because 'all Scripture is inspired by God' (2 Tim. 3:16
GNB, NJB) and 'the prophets did not think these things up
on their own, but they were guided by the Spirit of God'
(2 Pet. 1:21 CEV), those who wish to read these Scriptures
should depend on the same Holy Spirit, so that the Lord
should 'open their minds to understand the Scriptures'
(Lk. 24:45 REB, GNB, NJB). Before reading, we could pray
in words like these:

'Take the veil from my eyes, that I may see
The wonder to be found in your law' (Ps. 119:18 REB).

But clearer spiritual understanding of God's Word to mankind should lead to the intended response of faith. John wrote: '. . . these [miracles] are written so that you will put your faith in Jesus as the Messiah and the Son of God. If you have faith in him, you will have true life.' (Jn. 20:31 CEV)

But '*faith* without *actions* is dead' (Jas. 2:26 GNB) 'Do not deceive yourselves by just *listening* to his word; instead, *put it into practice*. . . . if you *look closely* into the perfect law that sets people free, and *keep on paying attention* to it and do not simply listen and then forget it, but *put it into practice—you will be blessed by God in what you do*.' (Jas. 1:22, 25 GNB2, my italics)

Bibliography

References to versions of the Bible, etc. are to be found in chapter 1: Tables 1–3, in chronological order; they also appear in alphabetical order in the Index.

For reviews of versions, consult Lewis's book for extensive listing.

Reviews of the 1985 edition of this book (Duthie: B T) are noted against the relevant journal titles.

Current reference books on Bible versions are in bold type.

Anderson, G W & D E: *What today's Christian needs to know about the NIV*, Trinitarian Bible Society, London, 1991?

Arena, Universities and Colleges Christian Fellowship.

Arena, 1986 (A T H Simons): Review of Duthie: B T.

Arichea, D C: 'Taking theology seriously in the translation task' (p 309–16) *TBT* 33.3, 1982.

Australian Church Record (D Kirk): Review of Duthie: B T.

Báez-Camargo, G: 'The Dead Sea Scrolls and the translator' *TBT* 31.4, 1980.

Bailey, L R (ed.), *The Word of God: a guide to English versions of the Bible*, Atlanta, 1982.

Baptist Times 1986: Review of Duthie: B T.

Bascom, R A : Review of Tov (p.155–6) *TBT* 45.1, 1994.

Beekman, J: 'Idiomatic translations and some underlying theological questions' (p.8–17) *NOT* 68, 1978.

Beekman, J & Callow, J & K: *Translating the Word of God I–II*, Zondervan, Grand Rapids, 1974.

Believers Magazine (T W): Review of Duthie: B T.

Blight, R C: 'Section headings' (p.26–31) *NOT* 75, 1975.

Bratcher, R G: Review of 'NIV—the Bible of evangelicals' (p.345–50) *TBT* 30, 1979.

Bratcher, R G: Review of Schonfield 1985 (p.339–41) *TBT* 38.3, 1987.

Bratcher, R G: Review of the REB (p.342–8) *TBT* 43.3, 1992.

Bratcher, R G: Review of Gaus' Unvarnished New Testament (p.147–9) *TBT* 44.1, 1993.

Bratcher, R G: Review of Hargreaves (p.151–3) *TBT* 46.1, 1995.

Bratcher, R G: Review of Peterson NT (p.154–5) TBT 46.1, 1995.

Bruce, F F: *History of the Bible in English*, Lutterworth, London, 1961, 1970, 1979.

Bruce, F F: Review of Duthie: *Bible Translations TBT*.

Bruce, F F: 'What does it mean?' (p.41–52) in Polkinghorne (ed.).

Bruggen, J Van: *The Future of the Bible*, Nelson, Nashville, 1978.

Bullard, R A: 'Feminine and feminist touches in the Centenary NT', *TBT*.

Buzz Magazine: Review of Duthie: B T.

Carson, D A: *The King James Version Debate*, Baker, 1979.

Carson, D A: 'The limits of dynamic equivalence in Bible translation' (p.200–13) *ERT* 9.3, 1985.

Chilton, B D: 'Which translation?' in *Beginning New Testament Study*, SPCK, London, 1986.

Chow, P K: 'Analogical applications of information theory to semantic problems' (p.310–8) *TBT* 31.3, 1980.

Christian Brethren Research Fellowship Journal.

Christian Graduate, Inter-Varsity Fellowship, London.

Christian Literature World, Sovereign Grace Trust, Lafayette IN.

Church Review (C O'Shea): Review of Duthie: B T.

Church Times (Joseph Robinson): Review of Duthie: B T.

Clark, D: 'Culture then and now' (p.95–105) in Polkinghorne (ed.).

Clark, D: 'The Dead Sea Scrolls and Isaiah' (p.122–30) *TBT* 35.1, 1984.

Clark, D: 'Problems in Bible translation' I–III, *H*, 1981.

Comfort, P W: *Early Manuscripts and Modern Translations of the New Testament*, Wheaton, 1990.

Crim, K R: 'The New Jewish Version of the Scriptures' (p.148–52) *TBT* 26.1, 1975.

Custer, S & Neal, M: *A critical analysis of a dangerous scriptural perversion* (GNB/TEV), Greenville, 1970, 82.

Deer, D: 'Supplying "only" in translation' (p.227–34) *TBT* 38.2, 1987.

Dennett, H: *Graphic Guide to Modern Versions of the New Testament*, Bagster, 1965.

Dennett, H: 'Problems in Bible translation' (p.19–22) *CBRFJ* 1968.

Dillard, R E: 'Translators, translations, and the church' *NOT* 60, 1975.

Duthie, A S: *Bible Translations and How to Choose between Them*, Paternoster, Exeter, 1985.

Duthie, A S: 'Semantic structure and translation' (p 25–36) *NOT* 1983.

Edwards, E G: 'On using the textual apparatus of the UBS Greek NT' (p.121–42) *TBT* 28.1, 1977.

Ellington, J: 'Can pronouns be divine?' (p.223–30) *TBT* 43.2, 1992.

Ellington, J: 'Taboo words in the Bible' (p.232–4) *TBT* 44.2, 1993.

Ellington, J: 'Wit and humor in Bible translation' (p.301–13) *TBT* 42.3, 1991.

Elliott, J K: Review of P W Comfort (p.343–5) *TBT* 42.3, 1991.

Elliott, P & Andrews, J S: 'In defence of the NEB' *H*, 1979.

Ellingworth, P: Review of *Anchor Bible Dictionary* (p.144–6) *TBT* 44.1, 1993 & (p.354–6) *TBT* 44.3, 1993.

Ellingworth, P: Summary of Epp (p.141–2) *TBT* 31.1, 1980.

Ellingworth, P: 'Twelve pillars of wisdom? Bible translation' (p.8–11) *Arena* 1988.

Epp, E J: 'Jews and Judaism in the *Living New Testament*' (p.80–96) in Tuttle (ed.).

Expository Times: Review of Duthie: B T.

Evangelical Quarterly, Paternoster Press (I H Marshall): Review of Duthie: B T.

Evangelical Review of Theology, World Evangelical Fellowship.

Evangelical Times.

Family (Paul Merton): Review of Duthie: B T.

Fanning, B M: *Verbal Aspect in New Testament Greek*, Oxford, 1990.

Fee, G D: 'The Majority Text and the original text of the NT' (p.107–18) *TBT* 31.1, 1980.

Fee, G D & Stuart, D: *How to Read the Bible for all its Worth*, Zondervan/Scripture Union, 1982/3.

Fehderau, H W: 'Quality control of Bible translations', *NOT* 75.

Floodtide (V P): Review of Duthie: B T.

Foster, L: *Selecting a Translation of the Bible*, **Standard, Cincinnati, 1983.**

Freedman, D N (ed.): *The Anchor Bible Dictionary*, Doubleday, New York, 1992.

Fry, E: 'Translating biblical measurements' (p.237–43) *TBT* 29.2, 1978.

Fry, E: 'The use and value of section headings in printed scriptures' (p 235–9) *TBT* 34.2, 1983.

Giese, R L jr: ' "A place for everything and everything in its place": the role of range and sense in Bible translation' (p.301–309) *TBT* 44.3, 1993.

Glassman, E H: *The Translation Debate*, **IVP, Downers Grove, 1981.**

Gordon, R P: 'Versions ancient and modern', *H*, 1979.

Green, J P (ed.): *Christian Literature World*.

Green, J P & Johnston, P J: *Unholy Hands on the Bible II*, Sovereign Grace Trust, Lafayette IN, 1991; 'A critique of all modern versions'—*from a grossly uninformed viewpoint (ASD)*.

Gross, C: Review of Fanning, *TBT* 44.3 93.

Hammond, G: *The Making of the English Bible*, Carcanet, Manchester, 1982.

Hargreaves, C: *Translator's freedom—Modern English Bibles and their Language*, JSOT, Sheffield, 1993.

Harvester, Paternoster Press, Exeter, 1986 (John Peters): Review of Duthie: B T.

Hess, H: Letter (p.29–31) *NOT* 109, 1985.

Hohulin, L: 'Readability, and linguistic complexity in translation' (p.14–28) *NOT* 91, 1982.

Hohulin, R M: 'Inspiration, authority, and reliability' (p.3–10) *NOT* 91, 1982.

Jones, J L: *But* **Which** *Bible?* **Bible Reading Fellowship, London, 1978, 1981.**

Kee, H C (ed.): *The Bible in the Twenty-first Century*, American Bible Society, New York, 1993.

Kraft, C H: 'What is God trying to do?' *NOT* 72, 1977.

Kubo, S & Specht, W F: *So Many Versions? Twentieth Century Versions of the Bible*, **Zondervan, Grand Rapids, 1975, 1983.**

Levi, P: *The English Bible 1534–1859*, Constable/Eerdmans, 1974.

Lewis, J P: *The English Bible from KJV to NIV—a history and evaluation*. Baker, Grand Rapids, 1981,1991.

Lode, L: 'The presentation of new information' (p.101–8) *TBT* 35.1, 1984.

Loewen, J A: 'A new look at section headings in West African translations' (p.237–41) *TBT* 36.2, 1985.

Loewen, J A: 'Who am I translating for?' (p.201–4) *TBT* 37.2 1986.

Louw, J P: *Meaningful Translation: its implications for the reader*, United Bible Societies, 1992.

Macgregor, G: *The Bible in the Making*, John Murray, London, 1959.

Macleod, D: 'Received or rejected? The text behind your version', *ET* Feb 1980.

Martin, C G: 'The public image of the Bible' (p.115–22) in Polkinghorne (ed.).

Methodist Annotated Booklist 1986: Review of Duthie: B T.

Meurer, S: 'Theological considerations about the distribution of selections', *TBT* 32.3, 1981.

Mombert, J I: *English Versions of the Bible*, Bagster, 1883, 1907.

Moore, R K: 'The doctrine of "justification" in the English Bible at the close of the twentieth century' (p.101–16) *TBT* 45.1, 1994.

Mundhenk, N: 'What translation are you using?' *TBT* 25.4, 1974.

New Testament Abstracts 1986: Review of Duthie: B T.

Newell, A G: 'Too many modern versions?' (p.227–36) *EQ* 53.4, 1981.

Newman, B M: 'Biblical poetry and English style' (p.405–411) *TBT* 44.4, 1993.

Newman, B M: 'Some hints on solving textual problems' (p.430–5) *TBT* 33.4, 1982.

Newman, B M: 'The old way and the new way' (p.201–7) *TBT* 28.2, 1977.

Newman, B M: 'Readability and the NIV of the NT' (p.325–36) *TBT* 31.3, 1980.

Nida, E A: *Bible Translating*, United Bible Societies, 1961.

Nida, E A: *God's Word in Man's Language*, Harper, 1952.

Nida, E A: *Good News for Everyone*, Word Books, Waco TX, 1977.

Nida, E A: 'The "harder reading" in textual criticism—an application of the second law of thermodynamics' (p.101–7) *TBT* 32.1, 1981.

Nida, E A: 'Quality in translation' (p 329–32) *TBT* 33.3, 1982.

Nida, E A: *Toward a Science of Translating*, Brill, Leiden, 1964.

Nida, E A: & Taber, C R: *The Theory and Practice of Translation*, Brill, Leiden, 1969.

Notes On Translation, Summer Institute of Linguistics, Dallas.

Omanson, R L: 'Perspectives on the study of the NT text' (p.107–23) *TBT* 34.1, 1983.

Omanson, R L: 'What's in a name?' (p.109–19) *TBT* 44.4, 1989.

Omanson, R L: Review of the NRSV with Apocrypha (p.337–41) *TBT* 42.3, 1991.

Omanson, R L: Review of the New Oxford Annotated Bible . . . (p.352–4) *TBT* 44.3, 1993.

Osborn, N D: 'Basic types of footnotes for OT translations' (p.414–8) *TBT* 33.4, 1982.

Osborn, N D: 'The Name: when does it make a difference?' (p.415–22) *TBT* 43.4, 1992.

Paisley, I R K: *The Antichrist Bible* (REB): *an exposure*, Belfast, 1989.

Partridge, A C: *English Biblical Translation*, Deutsch, London, 1973.

Passantino, B & G: Review of Riplinger (p.38–42) *Cornerstone* 23(104), 1994.

Payne, D F: *Modern Translations of the Bible*, Pickering & Inglis, Glasgow, 1973.

Polkinghorne, G J (ed.): *The Bible in the Eighties*, =CBRF J 31–2.

Pope, H: *English Versions of the Bible*, Herder, St Louis, 1952.

Pritz, R: 'Cross references' (p.201–5) *TBT* 41.2, 1990.

Purkis, R: *The English Bible and its Origins*, Angel, Chichester (UK), 1988.

The Reaper (NZ): Review of Duthie: B T.

Reform (Roger Tomes): Review of Duthie: B T.

Reformed Review 43.4, 1990: on 'Modern English translations of the Bible'

Reformed Theological Review (J W Woodhouse): Review of Duthie: B T.

Reiss, K: 'Understanding a text from the translator's point of view' (p.124–34) *TBT* 32.1, 1981.

Riplinger, G A: *New Age Bible Versions: an exhaustive documentation exposing the message, men and manuscripts moving mankind to the Antichrist's One World Religion*, AV, Ohio, 1993.

Robertson, E H: *The New Translations of the Bible*, SCM, London, 1959.

Rye, J: 'Can they understand you?' *ET* 1980.

R B Salters, Review of The Writings: Kethubim ... (NJV) (p.142–3) *TBT* 35.1 1984.

Sangster, D: 'Did Jesus spell "me" with a capital M?' (p.48–50) *CG* 1974.

Sanneh, L: *Translating the Message: the Missionary Impact on Culture*, Orbis, Maryknoll NY, 1989.

Scanlin, H P: 'The presuppositions of HOTTP and the translator' (p.101–16) *TBT* 43.1, 1992.

Search (Richard Clarke): Review of Duthie: B T.

Seek (RSA) 1986 (John Carter): Review of Duthie: B T.

Sheehan, B: *Which Version Now?* Carey, Haywards Heath, 1980.

Sjölander, P: 'Expressing religious terms in simple language' (p.426–31) *TBT* 34.4, 1983.

Sjölander, P & Rye, J: 'How clear is a simplified version?' (p.223–9) *TBT* 33.2, 1982.

Smith, J: 'Footnotes and glossaries' (p.414–20) *TBT* 42.4, 1991.

Society of OT Studies Booklist (R J Coggins): Review of Duthie: B T.

Sollamo, R: 'The source text for the translation of the OT' (p.319–22) *TBT* 37.3, 1986.

Southwestern Journal of Theology (Finlay Graham): Review of Duthie: B T.

Sovereign Grace Trust: *Perspective*.

The Bible Translator, United Bible Societies; 1986 (F F Bruce): Review of Duthie: B T.

Thomas, K J: Review of Sanneh (p.151–3) *TBT* 43.1, 1992.

Thompson, J A: 'Bible geographies and atlases and their use in translating' (p.431–7) *TBT* 32.4, 1981.

Tov, E: *Textual Criticism of the Hebrew Bible*, Fortress, Minneapolis, 1992.

Tuttle, G A (ed.): *Biblical & Near Eastern Studies. Essays in honor of W S LaSor*. Eerdmans, 1978.

Vance, L M: *A Brief History of English Bible Translations*, Pensacola, FL, 1993.

Vaughan, C: *The New Testament in Twenty-six Translations*, Zondervan, 1967.

Vidyajyoti (P M Meagher): Review of Duthie: B T.

Vox Reformata (S V): Review of Duthie: B T.

Waard, J de & Nida, E A: *From One Language to Another. Functional equivalence in Bible Translating*, Nelson, Nashville, 1988.

Walden, W: *Guide to Bible Translations*, Livingworks, Boston, MA, rev.1991.

Weigle, L A: *The English New Testament from Tyndale to Revised Standard Version*, Nelson, 1950.

Wendland, E R: 'Receptor language style and Bible translation II' (p.319–28) TBT 32.3, 1981.

Wilt, T L: 'Alphabetic acrostics: perhaps the form can be represented', TBT 44.2, 1993.

Wonderly, W: *Bible Translations For Popular Use*, United Bible Societies, 1968.

Zogbo, L: 'Writing introductions to books of the Bible' (p.228–30), TBT 41.2, 1990.

Index

Author names (see also Bibliography); important terms, main scripture references; versions of Bible and of NT and OT; Bible version abbreviations (see also Tables 1–3 of chapter 1).